I<small>T</small> W<small>A</small>

IT WAS A MIRACLE

*Stories of Ordinary People
and Extraordinary Healing*

Kamila Blessing

Augsburg
MINNEAPOLIS

For Tati

Scripture quotations, unless otherwise noted, are from The Holy Bible, New International Version, copyright © 1973, 1978, 1984 International Bible Society. Used by permission of Zondervan Bible Publishers.

Scripture quotations marked NRSV are from New Revised Standard Version Bible, copyright © 1989 by the Division of Christian Education of the National Council of the Churches of Christ in the U.S.A. Used by permission.

Cover photo by Tony Stone Images. Used by permission.
Cover design by Craig Claeys.
Book design by Michelle L. Norstad.
Edited by Ann Rehfeldt.

Library of Congress Cataloging-in-Publication Data
Blessing, Kamila, 1948–
    It was a miracle : stories of ordinary people and extraordinary
healing / by Kamila Blessing.
        p. cm.
    Includes bibliographical references (p.).
    ISBN 0-8066-3732-3 (alk. paper)
    1. Spiritual healing. I. Title.
BT732.5.B57 1999
234'.131—dc21   98-49504
                                                            CIP

The paper used in this publication meets the minimum requirements of American National Standard for Information Sciences—Permanence of Paper for Printed Library Materials, ANSI Z329.48-1984.   ♻ ™

Manufactured in the U.S.A.   AF-9-3732

03   02   01   00   99   1   2   3   4   5   6   7   8   9   10

Table of Contents

Preface: A Word about the People and Events in This Book 7

1. My Own Introduction to Prayer for Healing 9

2. Healing in the Gospels: The Essential Credential 15

3. Grace, Forgiveness, and Healing 31

4. Faith Development, Fear of God, and Healing 39

5. A New Heart 49

6. Bridging the Gap 57

7. Finding the Father in Heaven 67

8. The Place of Praise in Healing 73

9. Gabriel, Child from Heaven 83

10. Paul's Hanky 89

11. Two Resurrections 99

12. Manna Faith Manifest: Healing Sustenance 107

13. Inner Healing: Your Body Is the Temple of the Holy Spirit . . . 115

14. Shattered Spirits, Hungry Lives 123

15. Arise and Shine: A Burst of Joy for the Brokenhearted 131

16. Vindication 139

17. Resurrection Tree 145

18. The Bottom Line 155

Postscript 159

A Word about the People and Events in This Book

To my knowledge, every healing story in this book is true. I have changed the names of people and places as well as some minor details, however, in order to safeguard the privacy of those involved.

If you see your own healing story in these accounts, it is probably not you about whom I am writing. In looking back over many years of healing ministry, I am astonished at how often a seemingly unique set of circumstances will repeat. For example, the story in chapter 16 of my mother and the young man who had just received orders to ship out to Vietnam occurred in and around my home. Thus I know it to be true. Yet even that healing is not entirely unique: some years after those events, I read an almost identical story in another author's book about healing—an author whom my mother and I never knew. The account in chapter 4 is actually an amalgam of two stories: the original experience and another very similar one that occurred about two years later. In the chapter about Gabriel (chapter 9), I drew from the stories of numerous women who have called and asked me to pray for them to conceive a child or to help them deal with a miscarriage.

In a sense, all healings are unique, because everyone's relationship with the Lord is unique. That aspect of uniqueness has been carefully guarded here. I have taken great care that the privacy of the people in these stories be preserved. Only in the stories of my own healings have I identified the actual recipient of the healing.

For all the people who here remain anonymous, I have a deep love, because through them I have seen the Lord at work. I hope that you will too.

Chapter 1

My Own Introduction to Prayer for Healing

The fresh chicken stock was steamy hot, wonderfully appetizing, meaty and fragrant with the aroma of onion, parsley, carrot, celery, and rosemary. And I was pouring it down the drain. As I poured and poured, I kept thinking, "There's something wrong with this—though I can't figure out what exactly. There must be some use for something so delicious and with such an inviting smell." But there was nowhere to put it. Recently married, I had not yet acquired containers for storing voluminous things, such as this broth. Nor did the refrigerator in our little apartment in Pittsburgh have room for it. Regret and gustatory yearning well up even now as I remember the sight and smell of that rich broth being poured down the drain. Several hundred rich soups and gravies later, I know what I should have been doing with that lovely bouillon.

About five years after the chicken broth incident, I began receiving my first pastoral counseling. The counseling minister was deeply gifted in praying for healing and always ended our sessions with a brief prayer. Yet this prayer, though it came from the sincerest Christian I knew, always seemed perfunctory. I could hear only its shortness and formality. Straight from our church's prayer book, it came across as canned. It also made me uncomfortable, because it touched a spiritual place in me that was not ready to be shared. For me, praying was private. So one day at the end of a session with my counselor, I said, "Don't do that prayer thing at me anymore." Looking a little hurt, he only said, "Don't do that to me. Don't ever accept a prayer if you don't want it." While I expected him to be offended that I did not want the prayer, he was instead offended that I had ever allowed him to pray for me without my believing in his praying.

Many powerful healing prayers later, I am not only the recipient of healing, but I have become very comfortable with prayer for others. As with the incident of the chicken broth, I regret wasted opportunity—in this case, for healing prayer. At that moment I was not ready. As with the chicken broth, I did not yet know what to make of it. I was pouring out the opportunity for the prayers of another, all the while knowing I was going to wish I had not. I just could not place it in the pattern of my life right then.

If only someone had told me—and I had been able to receive—that "where two or three come together in my name, there am I [Jesus] with them" (Matthew 18:20), I would have known that my counselor had been offering a sort of "starter prayer." This prayer was intended to be—when I was ready—a signal that he was willing to offer me healing prayer of a more specific and richer nature. The healer himself, Jesus of Nazareth, would have been there in some special way to receive those prayers even before I was ready for him or aware of his presence. If only I hadn't said that I did not want those prayers!

My inability to involve another person in prayer came about in part because I had never experienced anyone praying with me before, so naturally I was uncomfortable with it. From my first very real experience of God at age twelve, I had prayed for myself and others, but always by myself. God had been palpably present to me ever since that experience—when God answered, in a way I cannot really explain in rational terms, my question of whether there was a God. How could a person who has had such a powerful experience of God still throw out the healing prayers of a counselor? For me, the answer was that God was trustworthy, but people were not. I had carefully avoided praying with anyone or telling anyone about my prayer life. Communication with the Lord was too precious and sensitive an experience to expose to others' possible comments, and I did not want to let anyone in on my secret experience of Jesus.

I also was aware of a very serious and intractable contradiction between my own experience of God's presence and my experience of corporate religious practice. My Jesus did not seem to be a part of that corporate experience, but just as important, I was not part of it. When I was a child, the minister never once greeted me or said my name. I was not invited to the communion table because at that time children usually waited to commune until they were confirmed. No one explained the formal service to me. Because I was not part of the social aspect of worship, as a child or as a young adult, the decision to "go public" was extremely difficult.

How, then, did it finally happen? Going public was the direct result of counseling. Ever since that childhood experience of the presence of God, I had had a powerful yearning to celebrate God—specifically to celebrate the Eucharist, though more generally to express this powerful upwelling of the Spirit within me. My private experience of God had manifested itself all around me for nearly seventeen years. I had, for example, without training and without thinking too much about it, prayed for minor healings for myself and I had seen them occur. In adulthood, my desire to celebrate God drove me to counseling.

In my denomination, wanting to celebrate Eucharist meant seeking ordination. That was one of the things, therefore, about which I needed counseling. The irony was that my counselor did not believe in the ordination of women to the priesthood. I was unaware—innocent in the devoid-of-knowledge sense—of the women's movement and of the political ramifications of my wanting to be ordained. I simply had had this sense of calling for all of those years. It had taken firm root in me, and I kept having private experiences that confirmed the very immediate and loving presence of God with me.

One day, a mutual friend called this counselor and, without asking me, made an appointment for me to see him. I was not comfortable about it, but I felt obligated to go. And so it was that the most remarkable conversation I believe I have ever had came about. There I was, standing at the counselor's office door, face-to-face with him for the first time. I was taken off guard by his asking me rather stiffly, without "Hello" or any other preamble, "So why do you want to be ordained?" Innocently, but absolutely convinced of what I was saying, I replied, "Because God called me." The counselor's entire countenance changed. He seemed to relax. He kindly invited me in, and we began the most powerful series of conversations of my life, first about me and God, and then about me and my relationship with the world.

The miracle was that this man, unlike some others I have known in the years since, wanted to express the love of God much more than he wanted to keep distance from someone who opposed his own theological position. To the counselor, my position—as stated in my one chance to make a first impression on him—was a theological stance, rather than a political one. I myself would not have been able to state that then, but that was what made the difference to him. What also made a difference was that, evidently hungry for as much of God as he could get, he really believed, and showed his enjoyment of, my religious experiences.

By the time these conversations came to a natural end, I had opened my mouth and spoken my deepest, inner self. I was "unlocked." The spiritual deprivation of my church experiences was now matched by the opposite: a true communion with another Christian spirit.

Eventually, I did let him pray with and for me, and after some time I was also able to pray with and for other people. What happened within me during that time made that shared prayer possible. When I was twelve, it had become possible for me to pray because I had a certain ownership of faith and prayer. Then prayer was no longer only demanded by other people but was genuinely a part of myself. To progress to the next step of opening that part of myself to other people, I had to trust God to take care of the sensitive nature of that inner aspect of myself. That had been made possible by the counselor, a person whom I could trust absolutely not to step on or misuse my early spiritual experiences.

Thus the experience of turning down prayer was actually a turning point. When I began to consider the implications of sharing prayer, my private faith began to work in the world in a new way.

My experience of poured-out, wasted opportunities for healing has made me sensitive to the fact that many good people simply do not have ownership of shared faith or prayer. The concept that God is actually going to answer often seems strange, as it does to me still today. It is also thoroughly understandable that someone who has not experienced God as a loving presence may not be able to approach prayer, let alone prayer for healing. But how I wish I could prevent others from throwing out this powerful source of life-sustenance, at least long enough to see what it can do for them and for others. This, however, might well involve a change in the way they see themselves in relation to God and to other people.

This book is an invitation to drink deeply of the healing power of the Lord's presence. It is for those who pray, as well as for those who do not. At the end of each chapter, I have offered what I call "prayer starters." You can think of these as bread starters—the small bit of leaven which, with some additional ingredients of your own and a little patience, may lead to great spiritual sustenance. In the next chapter, "Healing in the Gospels: The Essential Credential," we will examine how we know, through the Scriptures, that spiritual healing is available to us today. The purpose of that chapter is to provide you with your own knowledge that such healings are a genuine, indeed a major, aspect of Christianity.

In subsequent chapters, I present stories of healing to which I can personally attest. This material—both the stories and the scriptural background—is for you, wherever you are in Bible knowledge and in awareness of spiritual healing. Most of the people in these stories were unaware of spiritual healing. They were simply needy enough to accept a gift of prayer. Perhaps their stories will provide a rich stock from which you too may feed, in your own way and in your own time.

Chapter 2

Healing in the Gospels: The Essential Credential

I n the history of medicine, we have many great stories and many great heroes. Lister contributed to surgery by showing that we needed to use antiseptics. Pasteur originated the germ theory of disease. Salk created the polio vaccine.

We worship the heroes of medicine because they seem to promise direct, visible results in the most insecure aspect of our life: our susceptibility to disease and early death. You can stay home, stay out of cars and airplanes, never go anywhere that is dangerous, and protect yourself as much as is humanly possible. You can do all of that and still be struck down by illness.

We still do not have a cure for the cold. (Who ever would have thought that going to the moon would be easier than curing the common cold?) Allergies are incurable—did you know that? And the threat of a living death is always with us. One quarter of us will be affected by cancer. One tenth of us will suffer from mental illness. We know a lot about the things that predispose a person to mental illness and we know a great deal about controlling its effects through drugs, but we do not know how to prevent it or cure it.

Beyond all of that, the very things that make us successful in our culture tend to kill us. Almost everybody knows that stress on the job is linked to hypertension and heart disease. Heart disease is still the number one killer, and a recent projection showed that this will still be true into the twenty-first century.

Perhaps just as telling is the recent interest in the medical community in the subject of holistic and spiritual healing. The scientific community is reaching for something beyond physical intervention. This development does not imply any put-down of the medical community or of medicine—rather, the reverse. It is a part of the progress medicine is making today to recognize the spiritual side of the human being and the fact that this side of us may be enlisted for healing. The type of healing about which you will read in this book is being acknowledged—even identified as a necessary component—by a significant portion of the medical community.

Now, before we go any further, I must pause to make a crucial point. According to the book of Ecclesiasticus (one of the books between the Old and New Testaments), there should not be any conflict between scientific healing and spiritual healing. There it says, "Honor physicians for their services, for the Lord created them; for their gift of healing comes from the Most High. . . . The Lord created medicines out of the earth, and the sensible will not despise them. . . . By them the physician heals and takes away pain; the pharmacist makes a mixture from them. God's works will never be finished; and from him health spreads over all the earth" (Ecclesiasticus 38:1, 4, 7-8 NRSV). Ultimately, all healing comes from God—including healing that comes by way of scientific medicine.

The point of view in this book is that scientific medicine is a good thing. (For this reason, I always send people to their physicians, particularly when we have seen a definite and miraculous healing. There is no harm in verifying spiritual healing.) But physical medicine may not be enough. Sometimes it is disastrously insufficient. Many physicians will tell you this same thing.

Is It Hopeless? Why We Need the Great Physician

If we cannot absolutely count on scientific medicine, is the health situation hopeless? No, because there is one physician who can heal any illness, even death. He does it by means of a direct change in you and by altering the meaning as well as the outcome of the suffering in our lives. That physician is Jesus. Many people, even today, think that "the great physician" is just a cliché referring to a time in the past when a man called Jesus went around doing miracles. A whole theological point of view called "dispensationalism" says that miracles did once happen—but only then, not now. Some scholars think the stories of healing in the Bible don't really belong and that they are a myth, part of a traditional hero story.

But there was an actual Jesus. He was a historical figure, mentioned in the works of Josephus, a Palestinian Jew who worked as a historian for Caesar in first-century Rome. The Gospels tell us that Jesus did heal, and we have no historical records that contradict that assertion. Just as important, at the end of Mark's Gospel we are told that healing does not remain something of the past. In Mark 16:17-18, Jesus says, "These signs will accompany those who believe: In my name . . . they will place their hands on sick people, and they will get well." The Epistle of James says the same thing, commanding us to carry out spiritual healing (James 5:13-16).

Healing was the whole point of Jesus' coming—the healing and changing of people's lives at all levels of existence. To see this, you only need to think about the word salvation. In Greek, the language in which the New Testament is written, the word for "salvation" is always *sozo*. Sozo means "save," but in common usage it also means to heal, to save from deadly illness. In English, we have the word salve, which looks a lot like the word salvation. Yet it refers to a medicine. We also have salvage, to save from destruction, to bring about the literal salvation of something we care about. In Greek, "to save" is similarly connected with the idea of healing. To save is to save from being sick, to save from being death-ridden, and to save from destruction.

If we think Jesus came only to bring some ethereal, invisible afterlife, what we are saying is this: we are in the "salvation" business—but we claim only half of what Jesus offers us. We want the invisible, unprovable part but not the part that can help us on this earth. Nowhere in the Gospels does it say that Jesus came to save people's souls. That would imply merely souls. So why do we think that that is all he came to do? We have a right to the whole thing, the total salvation that the Gospels proclaim. That was the message of the Gospel story—that Jesus came to sozo us, to save us—mentally, physically, and spiritually.

Why does this misunderstanding persist? We are heirs of Greek culture and of a Western, rational mode of thought that has been superimposed upon the teachings of Jesus. But Jesus came from the Hebrew culture. And the Hebrew and Greek cultures saw the world differently. Many of the Greeks thought the human being was a spirit unfortunately trapped inside a body, and the two things—body and spirit—were essentially different from each other. But to the Hebrews, there is only the person, one whole, indivisible human being. If you read the Old and New Testaments—Paul's letters, for example—you surely see words in English that say "body," "spirit," and "soul." But from the Judaic perspective, and even among some of the Greeks, those are aspects of one totally integrated and unified personhood. In Greek, as in English, there simply were not words that could express the total unity of the human being and make it clear that this is what was intended. But to Jesus and to Paul and other writers of the New Testament, the inseparability of the human being, body and all, was an unquestioned reality.

We like to ask, when the body dies, what part of the person does God save out for himself? I have seen people get themselves extraordinarily confused in trying to tack down exactly what part of us gets salvaged after we die. For Christians, the point of reference is the Bible, and the Bible tells us what God saves: the "resurrection body." Read 1 Corinthians 15 closely and you will have a whole new view of the body and of what Paul was thinking when he wrote about salvation. He says that the earthly body and the heavenly body are different in nature, but the whole person is preserved in a whole new (resurrection) body. Like Jesus' body after the resurrection, all of us survives. Jesus went through the locked doors somehow, but then he showed the disciples his wounded hands and the spear wound in his side. He ate with them, the same fish they were eating. It was the same Jesus. The same, yet now invulnerable to death.

To put it another way, according to biblical teaching you cannot separate the essential aspects of a person. This concept involves a paradox that Paul deals with in 1 Corinthians 15. Surely the physical body disintegrates after our death. Yet somehow God sees us as one, inseparable being, which is our essential self. Paul's analogy is of a grain of wheat. You plant it and the seed dies, but the wheat plant comes up. So actually, even if the hull of the seed crumbles into the earth, the whole plant is still there, and more, it is a living being. It is the whole, the plant. Paradoxical as it seems, Jesus came to save the whole, essential self of each one of us—not just a part of us. Sometimes that includes saving our physical body while we need it to fulfill our life here. More often than you might ever guess, we have a foretaste of the healing of the total self in the form of the healing of illness or injury.

To be sure, a part of salvation is invisible to us on earth. In fact, Jesus uses his healings and miracles as an audiovisual aid to show people what more God has to offer them. The usual scene is this: Jesus heals, miraculously feeds five thousand people, or does some other miracle, and only then do the crowds follow him, and only then do they listen to his teaching. They see the miracle before they even know to believe in him. The healings are his way of demonstrating God's power and also of getting our total attention.

The Essential Credential

For the above reasons, one-fifth of the verses in the Gospels are devoted to healings. There are thirty-one references to healings or stories about healings. In all, about one-third of the Gospels is taken up by healing. It is not a minor subject.

Jesus made it clear that healing was—for the Messiah—what I call the essential credential. John the Baptist sent some people to him to ask, "Are you the one who was to come?" (Matthew 11:3). By this John meant, "Are you, Jesus, the Messiah?" Jesus replied, "Report to John what you hear and see: The blind receive sight, the lame walk, those who have leprosy are cured, the deaf hear, the dead are raised, and the good news is preached to the poor" (Matthew 11:4-5; see also Luke 4:16-21). That is the one proof John needed and the only qualification Jesus offered. This list of types of healing comes from Isaiah (Isaiah 61:1-2), and it was an accepted description of the credentials of the genuine Messiah.

Jesus also made it clear that his followers were to do the same kinds of healing. Whenever he sent out the disciples to preach, he also told them to heal. And they did. We see that in the story of the formation and growth of Christianity after the resurrection, a story found largely in the book of Acts. The disciples continued to use miraculous healing—just as Jesus had done—as evidence of the truth of Jesus' promise of salvation.

We can take encouragement from the accounts of their healing as well as from the story of their failure to heal. When they tried to cast a demon out of a boy and failed, they had to ask Jesus for help. Remember, in the Gospels the disciples—like us—are still learning. Like them, we can always learn more about healing and about the ways of coming closer to God. The truly important thing in understanding healing in the Bible is this: Christianity was brought about by Jesus and then by these disciples, who demonstrated the power of the Holy Spirit through healing.

What Kind of Healing?

What kind of healing did Jesus do? The hardest kind. In general, there are three kinds of healing: physical (including functional and organic), emotional, and ethical. Among physical ailments, a functional illness means something in the body doesn't work right but the function could be restored. For example, when Jesus healed the man who was paralyzed (Matthew 9), it was a physical healing, probably of a functional illness. The man's limbs were there, but they simply did not work. Organic illness means that part of the body is defective or sick and more is needed than just to make it work right again. The emotional is what we would call psychological. Ethical relates to morality. In all of the Gospels, there are only two ethical healings, the woman at the well (who had had many husbands) and Zacchaeus (who, because of Jesus, decided to stop extorting money from people).

The healings Jesus most often brought about were the kinds that are still a mystery for modern medicine: the organic, where something is really wrong with the body so it cannot do its work, and the psychological. The healing of the man with the withered hand (Matthew 12:10-13) is in the organic category of physical healing.

What about psychological healing? Jesus, while on the cross, presented his mother and his disciple John to each other as a new mother-son "family." That was in the category of emotional healing, even though the text does not tell us how she felt afterward. We do know that the terrible fear felt by the disciples after the crucifixion was replaced by joy and confidence when they saw the resurrected Jesus. Though the resurrection itself is the focus of the story, we should not overlook the fact that an emotional healing of enormous proportions also took place.

And what about mental illness? First, I want to make it clear that it is never appropriate to say something is "just" psychological. There may just be spiritual powers that attack us, hold on, and make our lives miserable. Evil spiritual forces may be one source of a tormented mind. The healing of the possessed man in the synagogue in Mark 1:23-26 is a good example. Another is the healing of the young boy in Matthew 17:14-18. In most translations, the boy is said to be "epileptic." However, the Greek word means "moonstruck"—literally, "lunatic." (Ancient peoples thought that epilepsy came from the influence of the moon, which is the reason for the translation "epileptic.") The story goes on to say that the boy was cured when Jesus cast the demon out of him. Here, if we take the text literally, we have a genuine healing of madness as well as an exorcism. For this reason, I am going to include exorcisms among the psychological healings. One thing we know: the Gospels tell us that those who had been possessed were completely healed. They never returned to Jesus for a further cure of the same thing.

The critical point is that Jesus tackled the most difficult of all healings. Jesus pointedly took on the worst sickness of all: the wearing out of our bodies, our mortality. In some cases he resurrected people, and resurrections in this life still happen today. I have seen more than one. Other times, the resurrection we receive is the eternal kind. We can't see the healing that is eternal life, but we have the demonstration project of the healings and miracles that Jesus and his disciples performed.

Jesus never turned anyone away. There is no doubt that Jesus did heal. There is also no doubt that everyone is invited to ask for healing.

The Why: A Whole-Bible View

"WHY NOT?" THE WRONG FIRST QUESTION

As you launch into the stories of healing in these chapters, no doubt you will be asking yourself—as everyone does—why does healing sometimes occur when we pray for it and sometimes it does not? The answer to the "why not" question is this: it's the wrong question—at least, the wrong first question. For one thing, it focuses on the negative. It assumes that God has not healed and that you will know the healing when you see it or will receive the healing in the way and at the time you desire. Human imagination is limited, and we should not presume that we know all of the ways in which God can heal.

For example, I prayed for twenty-five years for a physical healing of a skin problem I had, a healing that doctors had not been able to bring about. The entire time, I wondered why God did not heal it. I was frustrated because, in the meantime, I experienced a number of other healings in myself and in other people. Then one day I did receive the healing. Afterward, I looked at when this occurred and what other healings took place at the same time and realized with considerable surprise that the physical healing was tied to many other things within me. It needed to wait for, and was also a trigger for, certain very profound healing changes in my personal life. Sometimes even death can be a healing. There are several stories in this book that illustrate that. The point is, God is working on your need, in God's time and in God's way.

The second reason not to focus on the negative is that people often pronounce reasons for the lack of healing that end up causing great harm. One of the most frequent is "You (or I) must not have had enough faith." Sure enough, there are specific healings in the Gospels wherein the healed persons are told their faith has made them well. There are also passages in which Jesus says that the disciples have had too little faith for healing to take place (for example, Matthew 17:19-20). However, most of the healings are not accompanied by such statements.

It is not appropriate to assume that all healings require some amount of faith. The point is made strongly in the story of the man who asks for a healing for his son while making it clear that he has little confidence in Jesus. He says to Jesus, "If you can do anything . . . help us" (Mark 9:22). Even after Jesus' assurance, the father remains uncertain. Being desperate, however, he cries out, "Help me overcome my unbelief" (Mark 9:24). In this case, desperation brought him to Jesus and made him open to Jesus' healing activity. Often, desperation is an invitation, and it is always an opportunity, for the Lord to enter into our lives. When we think that even God cannot help us—but we are desperate enough to pray—that is (paradoxically) one of the moments when the Lord has the most access to whatever in us requires healing.

Of course, Jesus did heal the son of the man in Mark 9; the father's lack of faith was no barrier to healing. The healings and miracles were Jesus' way of attracting people's attention so that they would then listen to the message of the kingdom of God.

The point of the vast majority of healings was to give people an opportunity—for many of them, their first opportunity—to move on to faith in Jesus. Healing often comes first, then faith.

Thus people should not come away from a healing service feeling that they just didn't have enough faith. Nor is it ever appropriate to say or believe that someone is too sinful to be healed. Jesus healed many people and then said, "Sin no more." In those instances, he healed first, then commanded holiness. It is important that we not assume that healing can be prevented by our limitations. Jesus had to come and show us the way to God because people could not and cannot do it for themselves. He came specifically because of our limitations. If Jesus was to be true to his own purpose in coming, the message of salvation and its audiovisual aids—the healings—could not depend upon people's limitations. This is the doctrine of grace—unearned mercy from God—which is central to Christian theology.

A third reason not to dwell on why God doesn't heal is this: Jesus promised that prayers in his name would be answered. He didn't say when or how. However, the act of praying is itself a crucial element in our relationship with God. It may itself be a sort of healing, a healing of the relationship between us and the Lord.

Having said all of this, I should state clearly that it is never appropriate to engage in denial. Maybe you are not at this moment healed of the thing that is threatening you or your relationships. That should be acknowledged. Some people, though, take this too far. They actually set their heart of hearts upon bitterness toward God. This is not healthy for them, and it is another reason not to dwell on the "why not" question.

Sometimes people who are consumed by bitterness actually experience healing without even knowing it. I knew a man who was bitter because his adult daughter was terribly sick with diabetes. As a result, she was unable to keep her two-year-old son. Her father, who had worked hard for many years, now had to bring up a baby and spend day after day in the hospital with his daughter—all this at the one time of his life when he should have had some relief. He was worn out, and he was mad about it.

One day I was called to the emergency room, where the daughter lay, "flat-lining." Her heart had been stopped for a full half hour. The seven doctors and nurses who were trying to resuscitate her asked me to pray for her. Laying on of hands is an important healing technique, but in that crowded room, all I could reach of the daughter was her big toe. "Can I hold onto her toe?" I asked.

They agreed, and so I held on and prayed. After a little while, her heart started. The doctors were physically shaken, wondering whatever could have started her heart. "It must have been the ice pack," someone suggested. It might well have been. But why did their many techniques, expertly administered, not work until the moment when prayer was sent up to save the patient?

The daughter recovered. And her brain, despite having been deprived of blood and oxygen for a dangerously long time, recovered. When I talked with her a couple of days later, she knew me and talked lucidly. Yet her father continued to be bitter. He missed the fact of God's intervention in his own family! (I wonder how many more healings may have occurred without his realizing it.) Certainly God was not absent from that family.

This resurrection account reminds us not to dwell in the negative. The biblical stance is to keep our minds open and our hearts expectant, without denying what hurts us. Then we wait and see what God will do.

The Object of Praying

Of course, there are things you can do to make yourself more available for and aware of healing. It is always appropriate to learn more about ways of praying and more about yourself and any way in which you may be holding the Lord away from you. Since we are not puppets and the Lord made us that way on purpose, God is probably not going to force something on you if, in your heart of hearts, you don't want it. Also, you can always enrich your experience of God by studying and trying prayer. So learn all you can about how to pray.

Just remember that it is your experience of God that you are enriching. There is an objective, nonhuman, other power doing the healing—God. Human experience, and emotion in particular, are not sufficient to sense all of God's activity. Our experience and our feelings are used by God, but they are like a very small wire trying to carry a very big electrical signal. It shorts out; it may appear that no signal gets through, or you may see only sparks. Our human "wires" do not have sufficient capacity, and so we may think that there is no power running through us when there is actually a great deal of it (which is another reason not to assume that healing isn't occurring).

As we improve our prayer life, it is important to understand what we are doing when we pray—as well as what we are not doing. The purpose of prayer is not to force God to heal us or to change God's mind. That idea comes from a misunderstanding of prayer. There are several things, very human things, that we are not doing when we pray. We are not praying to convince God of anything or to tell God something he does not already know. We also are not trying to prove anything to God. We certainly are not trying to come up to some standard of faith or personal goodness.

The main reason we pray is that the Lord asks us—commands us—to remain in a relationship with him, and praying is one way to do that. Praying about a specific need is giving freewill consent for God to have dominion over that part of our life. Our consent is an active being-in-Christ. For God's reasons, it is essential to our relationship with him. It is our own essential credential.

"WHY?" THE RIGHT QUESTION

This leads us to the important question of why God does heal. There is an overriding "why" that, in a sense, answers the "why not?" The reason of reasons given by God in the Bible is "For my name's sake." Put another way, "The reason the Son of God appeared was to destroy the devil's work" (1 John 3:8). These statements reveal a purpose that is more important than everything else to God: to bring the kingdom of heaven, to reclaim from the forces of evil God's dominion over all of the earth. Throughout the New Testament, specifically through Jesus and Paul, we see God carrying out his plan to call the whole world's attention to himself.

Having said all of that, I can now state that there is one overriding reason why God has not healed certain things yet. The Bible represents the entire history of the people of God as a struggle for dominion over the world. When the Bible says that Jesus came to destroy the work of the devil, it acknowledges that evil is a genuine force, that it is independent of us. We are dependent upon God to deliver us from it. In the Bible, evil is presented as less powerful than God but as something with which God nonetheless must contend. God is working on it and, the Bible tells us, God will win. In the meantime, every prayer and every commitment by the people of God—especially when it is difficult to see that God is present with us—is one more victory for God and the kingdom.

Ultimately, that is why it is important not to assume the absence of healing. We and God are working together on the healing of the world, and we must remain in expectant unity for this much larger purpose. Besides, this earth is not all there is. Your healing may be a glorious one in the kingdom to come. Don't miss the joy of that expectation while you remain in this life!

As to why God does heal, then: he does so to invite you into his presence, to make you hungry for God, and to give you a taste of the kingdom to come.

Our Relationship with God: Holy Boldness

Our relationship with God is like that of a nursing baby with his mother. The mother loves her baby unreasonably and allows nothing to get between her and her child. The baby sucks unquestioningly, with the simple expectation of being fed when hungry. That is the relationship between God and creation. Jesus himself expresses this relationship, for example, in Mark 10:15, where the believer is to be just like a child in his approach to the Lord.

Add to this that God is, after all, God. Not only is God in charge, but God is far bigger than any of us. Jesus promised, "Whatever you ask for in prayer, believe that you have received it, and it will be yours," (Mark 11:24); he encouraged us to cultivate a spirit of expectancy when we pray (see also John 10:38; 14:11). Elsewhere, Jesus instructed his followers to pray in his name, to invest themselves in him, and to grant him dominion over their particular situation.

Jesus unequivocally told his followers to keep praying and never give up. In Luke 18, the persistent widow asks and asks a judge for justice, and finally he gives it to her just to get rid of her. If a corrupt human judge grants justice, Jesus taught, the merciful God surely means to grant our requests.Thus healing prayer should be approached with what I call "holy boldness." Just ask for it. If it does not occur when or in the way in which you asked, that does not mean that God did not hear you. It may mean that this healing is going to take time. The story of the widow implies that consistent and persistent prayer may be required. Perhaps God wants you to dwell with him for a time in this healing.

Just as important, perhaps you are called to face into the illness or evil and expect the Lord's presence with you, in spite of it. That, too, is a part of God's program—defying evil, using our expectancy as a kind of retaliation against evil. It is like peaceful civil disobedience: a quiet, absolutely firm stand in the very face of—in protest of—what is most troubling to you. That is holy boldness. The word of salvation through Jesus is often characterized in just this way: "We have the word of the prophets . . . and you will do well to pay attention to it, as to a light shining in a dark place" until Jesus' final victory "dawns in your hearts" (2 Peter 1:19, emphasis mine).

The word is like a light. But the Word, Jesus, is not just like a light shining in a dark place. He said, "I am the light of the world" (John 9:5). Jesus declared that he is with us specifically for the dark places in our lives. That means there will be dark places until the kingdom is complete. In fact, those dark places are the reason for his coming.

The only caution, therefore, in approaching healing prayer is this: do not assume you have not been healed or that God has not been listening. Everything we know about Jesus the healer leads us to a state of holy expectancy—expectancy of what the Lord will do in our lives and the lives of those for whom we pray. So go for it. Ask for what you need, be the suckling baby, drink deeply of the Holy Spirit, and above all, know that God has resources far beyond what you or anyone can ask or imagine.

Prayer Starter

Cultivate a spirit of expectancy when you pray. Carry this over to the time between prayers. For example, wherever you are, ask God, "Where are you?" Don't expect an answer immediately (though you might get one). Instead look for God in everything and everyone around you, even in the people you don't like. If you make a habit of this, one day it will come to you that you have in fact encountered God in some very ordinary thing or event. Eventually you may begin to see God nearly everywhere. Make it a secret project to expect God in every situation, good, neutral, or bad. God promises, "You will . . . find me when you seek me with all your heart. I will be found by you" (Jeremiah 29:13-14).

Seeking God in this way also has beneficial side effects. Whenever you look for God in other people, you actually reformulate your whole approach to them. If done consistently, this greatly enriches your relationships.

Chapter 3

Grace, Forgiveness, and Healing

I once made a pastoral call to a middle-aged woman who expressed nothing but bitterness from the time I arrived at her door. It was a bitterness, it seemed, rooted in a long-ago missed opportunity. As a young girl, she had had a chance to study nursing at a local hospital, but her father would not allow it. Women did not have professions, he argued; her pleadings went unheard. These many years later, she still could not forgive him for that, and seeing professional women brought up all of the old feelings again. She resented me and my work.

A short while later I learned the woman had died, with bitterness and unforgiveness the last things on her lips. She had literally made herself sick to death with unforgiveness. The injury done by her father was painful, but the injury done by herself was permanent.

I read about another woman who also harbored unforgiveness. She was to undergo major bowel surgery, because her X-rays indicated terrible disease. Before she went into the hospital, though, she went for counseling. As the counselor listened, he noted that there was one subject she never mentioned: her husband. He asked her about this. She hesitated. Finally, after much delay, she spoke of how much she hated her husband and about all of the things for which she could not forgive him. The counselor urged her to forgive him anyway since her surgery was so serious. Together they prayed to forgive the husband, and somehow the woman was able to do so. When she went to the hospital the next day, her presurgery X ray showed she that was perfectly healthy. She never had the surgery. Was this a coincidence? Of course. Was it also grace and divine healing? You bet.

These two stories address the biblical message about the relationship between evil, sin, and sickness. They also address the role of forgiveness—by God and by us—in healing. A great deal of illness, ours and others', can be healed through forgiveness on the human side, and by prayer for grace—God's gift of unmerited mercy—on the divine side. The combination of the two—our forgiveness and God's grace—is a powerful means toward healing. It is also an opportunity for us to participate in God's own program of redemption. In redemption, God forgives us. In forgiving others, we answer God back in kind. The Lord's Prayer says, "Forgive us our sins as we forgive those who sin against us," and in this type of healing, we carry that out.

This chapter does not deal with the person who deliberately sets out to do wrong but with the ways in which we become entangled, involuntarily, in the effects of the sin of the world. The two women in these stories did not set out to harm themselves, and they probably did not even reflect upon the sinfulness of their lack of forgiveness. They simply felt bad about their situations and could not seem to get out of them or leave them behind. They demonstrate the extent to which, intentionally or not, "all [of us] have sinned and fall short of the glory of God" (Romans 3:23). All of us are in need of forgiveness, and all of us need to be humble in handing out forgiveness to other people.

Consider the biblical view of the relationship between sin and sickness. In the Bible, illness is not necessarily the result of one's own sin. This is so even though there are instances in which Jesus heals a person and then says, "Go and sin no more." You have probably heard people say, "Since I'm sick, God must be punishing me." I cannot tell you how many times I have heard that from the patients I visit in hospitals. That is not the New Testament view, however. It is not even close. (This is something that is argued throughout the Old Testament but is clarified in the

New Testament.) We all know of young children who get cancer, too young to have had time to commit sin. In such cases, the evil in the world is like a spiritual air pollution that makes it hard for the most innocent baby to breathe. However, we can make ourselves sick, and unhealthy relationships such as those in the opening stories are among the ways in which we do so.

We participate in creating our own illness in various ways—some of them not what we would call sinful. For example, it is a general principle from family therapy that families and other close groups share a sort of pool of emotion and of emotional expression. In particular, there is usually one person who is the "expressor" of all of the family's tensions. Usually that is the most sensitive person, the most selfless and giving person in the family. That person is the family "shock absorber" and will often be the one who becomes mentally or physically sick. How many times have I heard people say, "Why Aunt Susie? She took care of everyone else all her life. She has been nothing but good. And she is the only one with cancer. It's so unfair!"

That is just exactly so. The one who is willing to take on everyone's hurts is going to be the one to express them. More often than you would think, the expression of tension is not direct, as in a verbal statement or a mean action. Much of the time the family's hurts are expressed through the truly caring person's health. This is a totally unconscious development, not under that person's control. She literally takes on the sin of the world as it is manifested in her own family. She also cannot recover under her own control unless she is taught some very specific means of spiritual and psychological recovery—or unless the family is changed to shift the locus of the expression of pain and stress.

A classic example is that of eating disorders. Family therapists have found that often the anorexic child of the family is expressing the emotional ill health of the family as a whole. The most common type of that emotional ill health is an overly controlling family member. The most vulnerable other person, often a young teenager, will unconsciously try to regain or redistribute the controlling influence in the family. The one thing over which the young person has control is eating, and so that is what "breaks." Not until the whole family is healed will this outwardly unhealthy behavior be remedied.

In such situations, no one sets out to commit any sin. Yet the whole family contributes to the young person's illness. Imagine the feelings that will come up when a family therapist shows how complex the relationships have been. Even if a true cure for the eating disorder is achieved, much forgiveness also needs to take place for the family to be truly and completely healed.

Sinful attitudes and actions, on one hand, and illness, on the other, are interlocked in complex ways. The degree to which we make a conscious contribution to ill health varies widely from one situation to another. On one end of the spectrum, we can willfully maintain poor relationships and attitudes—like the first woman I described. On the other end of the spectrum, the connection between the sinful side of relationships and the illness is completely unconscious and, in the absence of therapy, largely beyond anyone's control. This is the case with the eating disorder. In between is the type of situation in which an unhealthy attitude is maintained but is not necessarily a conscious decision. Instead, it is more like a human frailty. Such was probably the case with the woman who could not forgive her husband until she was helped to articulate the character of her marital relationship.

Fortunately, for such cases, there are two powerful means of healing, two kinds of forgiveness that can work miracles. Like sin, which has a spiritual and a human origin, forgiveness has a spiritual and a human origin. The more important by far is the spiritual: grace. God's loving kindness is available to anyone who asks. This is the New Testament principle. We have already quoted Romans 3:23, "All have sinned and fall short of the glory of God." This verse goes on to say that all "are justified freely by [God's] grace through the redemption that came by Christ Jesus." In other words, everybody "deserves" forgiveness, for no other reason than that Jesus earned it for us, in advance.

The second means toward healing consists in lending our own will and action to God's use through true, gracious forgiveness of other people. Of course, it is often easier to ask for grace than to feel forgiving, but the point is to forgive for God's sake, just as sincerely as you are able, whether you feel like it or not. God asks you to participate with him in eradicating the sin of the world. While you cannot tackle the whole task, you can deal with anything that has to do with you. You can do this in two ways: by asking God's forgiveness for any sin that is yours, and by freely offering forgiveness to anyone who sins against you.

Forgiving and asking forgiveness bring about obvious benefits. First, forgiveness itself is a healing. We all know instances of the healing of relationships when people forgive each other. We also know that repentance and asking for forgiveness can greatly relieve the emotional burdens we all carry around. And, as we have seen, forgiveness is an absolute necessity for our health. Grinding over bitterness and anger can and does make people sick, physically and mentally. "Protecting" yourself with resentment—keeping your guard up by not forgiving—is not a healthy way out. The healthy way is to allow Jesus Christ to be your advocate. And let go. It is what people call "enlightened self-interest."

Now, what if you just cannot bring yourself to forgive? Are you going to let go of this great resource and deny yourself its benefits? I hope not. There are two keys that are especially helpful in unlocking the power of forgiveness. The first is: seek to forgive. Look for opportunities to forgive rather than waiting for some desperate situation. Do not wait for a time when you are ready and willing to forgive in the natural course of things. Especially do not wait for the other person to do something first. Take charge, resolve to "be Jesus" for the other person, and make a deliberate choice to forgive. Remember, with Jesus, forgiveness is free. We too should not try to exact a price for forgiving another person.

The second key is to adopt an attitude of gratitude for God's grace in the situation and an attitude of understanding and forgiveness toward the other person. This is not easy. It takes some detachment. One way to do this is simply to tell the Lord, "Lord, I cannot and do not want to forgive this person. Help my unforgiveness." You also can pray to see at least one good and gracious thing in that person. Often you will find that the Lord will do surprising things within you if you only open the door of your heart, just a crack, to the possibility of forgiveness.

There are two reasons to do these things. One is humility. In principle, we are all sinners, and we need every connection to God's forgiveness that we can get. The other is, literally, for Christ's sake. With Christ, you are not alone. Indeed, with Jesus, you are rich in forgiveness and grace and can afford to be generous with your own forgiveness.

In a parish where I once worked, there was a particularly malicious older woman named Grace. Grace had never been heard to say anything but the most scathing denunciations to anyone, and because of her, a general sick atmosphere filled the coffee hours. One day the senior pastor, desperate about the situation, pleaded with me, "Kamila, please pray for Grace!"

I did. I prayed for Grace. I prayed for *grace*. And I **prayed** for grace. I needed lots of grace, because I also was afraid of Grace.

I decided what I had to do was to find a way in which I could forgive her. I had to try to find some way to see her in a positive light, so I began with an idea familiar to counselors: from Grace's point of view, her behavior must seem positive and constructive. I observed that her comments always concerned the way the parish was run. I also knew that Grace was just about the oldest member still active in keeping the altar appointments. Since that involved setting up bread, wine, and "dishes" for communion, this function was a highly charged equivalent to being the nurturer of the family.

A metaphor formed in my mind: in Grace's mind, Grace was the protecting mother. She was keeping things as they should be (read: as they always were). Therefore all change or potential change had to be fixed, or at least she had to speak up about it. It seemed only she was equipped to do this, since no one else was doing it. If she didn't, the parish would be sadly neglected or changed beyond repair.

I decided I would envision my mother in her place and answer everything she said—no matter how inappropriate it felt to me—as though she were my mother, protecting the family. I would try to respond in a way that did not directly address the thing she commented on but rather, her attitude about it—remembering that she probably thought of herself as a nurturer.

One Sunday, I found myself alone with Grace, significantly, in the parish kitchen. She complained, "The communion wine was all wrong today. Whoever bought that stuff is going to hear about it." I replied, "It's obvious you really care about the quality of worship in this church." At first she looked nonplused, but then her facial expression visibly softened and she replied, "Exactly. I want so much for it to be a rich experience for everybody." She left off any bitterness and talked about something else in a more normal tone. From the first time I did this, Grace continued to soften both her tone of voice and the subjects she brought up around me. In no time, she never said another negative word to me. It became a matter of some widespread comment that I was the only one who could actually talk with Grace—with grace. There was a spirit of forgiveness and more, of graciousness, between us.

At the next parish staff meeting, everyone asked me about my relationship with Grace. I explained what I had done. However, I found that the rest of the staff were just too afraid of Grace. They were unwilling to try my approach to her. They went on to further poor communication with her, though I went on to more good nurturing communication with her, and they commented on it. The parish-wide sickness caused by their unforgiving relationship with her continued.

We cannot afford unforgiveness. Unforgiveness is the worst medicine we can give ourselves. On the other hand, we can afford to be generous with forgiveness. Jesus promised us forgiveness, unbounded and unearned. Being generous with forgiveness, we are, ultimately, being generous with ourselves. We are bringing ourselves closer to God, participating in God's forgiveness, and becoming the agents, with the Lord, of healing. Through forgiveness, we become healers like Jesus, for ourselves and for other people.

Prayer Starter

Begin a program of inner closet-cleaning by praying regularly to forgive and be forgiven. This will make you more available to God for healing of relationships and healing of your own mind and body. Remember that God always cares for you, whatever your state of sin or unforgiveness. You cannot be turned down.

So, for example, you might pray:

Lord, forgive John for embarrassing me. I forgive him, too. Please forgive me for the way I reacted to him. Thank you, Lord, for the free gift of your forgiveness, and for being my surest protection from the things that hurt me. Amen.

Of course, when appropriate, ask the other person for forgiveness directly.

Chapter 4

Faith Development, Fear of God, and Healing

On one episode of the TV series M*A*S*H, the relationship between belief and healing in the New Testament was beautifully captured. In that episode, there was a soldier dying in the hospital tent, and Hawkeye was desperate because, medically, there was nothing more he could do. Then Father Mulcahy came into the tent. Hawkeye called to Mulcahy and said, "Come over here—we need a little cross action."

Father Mulcahy came and sized up the situation and said, "Okay, but I'm afraid it won't do much good." Then he took the soldier's hand and prayed for him to recover.

The soldier revived. Hawkeye said, "What's that you said about it not doing any good?"

Father Mulcahy looked puzzled and disconcerted. He said, "It's not supposed to work that way!" One almost had the feeling that Mulcahy wanted to run the other way—not from the suffering in the hospital tent, but from the evident intervention by God.

On M*A*S*H, the characters go at things pragmatically: if it works, do it. So naturally Father Mulcahy was not going to refuse to try anything that was suggested. Yet in this circumstance, he did not expect God actually to intervene. The ambiguity is intentional. As in so many scenes in that series, the moment of the healing was very poignant—and then it was over. The scriptwriters brought us all to the brink of a faith decision: did the prayer do it? Was it the hand-holding and the psychological warmth?

Was it a coincidence? Did God care, after all, in the middle of the wilderness of that war in Korea? But they leave off there, and we must come to our own conclusion.

I like this scene because it so accurately represents both the relationship between belief and many of the healings in the Bible as well as the place many of us find ourselves when we think about praying for healing. There are several reasons why even people of faith are not prepared for miracles, an important subject that this chapter addresses. At the end of this chapter, I will tell you a story of a miraculous healing that occurred among people who had even less experience of faith or miracles than the characters on M*A*S*H.

To begin, let us recall the place of faith in relation to healing. In chapter 2, I pointed out that the places where Jesus says to people, "Your faith has made you whole" are very specific passages not to be generalized to every other healing story. In the vast majority of the healings in the four Gospels, miracles come first and faith follows. In this chapter, I would like to take this reasoning another step. Like Father Mulcahy, we all have the need and the opportunity for our faith to grow a great deal. The first point we have to make here is that the Lord can and does reach out to us, wherever we are in our faith development. The second is that "the fear of the Lord" is supposed to be an awe of God—not a terror that makes you run away. Because so many people have misunderstood both of these points, each merits an extended discussion.

God will go to great lengths to demonstrate his caring for you—for the specific purpose of bringing you into closer communion with him. Luke 5, the story of the catch of fish, is a good example. In this story, Jesus uses a miracle to call his very first disciples. Look at the order in which things happen. The disciples-to-be are good Jews and faithful according to their own understanding of God and of their religion. They are not ignorant of matters of faith. Yet they evidently are not prepared for a miraculous intervention in the course of their ordinary, daily life.

In the story, these men have worked in their boats all night and caught nothing. Jesus tells Simon Peter and the others, "Put out into deep water, and let down the nets for a catch." Simon Peter objects but then relents, saying, "Because you say so!" But he means: "You're going to see just how foolish this is. I'm going along with you, but you'll see." How surprised the fishermen are when they actually catch some fish! And they don't catch just some fish. Luke describes the catch as so large that the nets begin to break, and the fishers have to get their friends to come and help them haul it all in. The first reaction of the disciples-to-be is fear, but Jesus reassures them: "Don't be afraid; from now on you will catch people." They drop everything and follow Jesus. People of some faith now have been given an experience which leads them to further faith, and to faith specifically in Jesus.

No one's faith is ever complete. There is always more, even for great people of faith. For example, most people associate Kathryn Kuhlman with miraculous healing. Yet even though for many years she was an evangelist who knew the Bible by heart, she did not discover that miraculous healing was available to us today until the middle of her career. It dawned on her one day while she was reading the Bible. Agnes Sanford, another great conveyer of God's power for healing, was the child of missionaries, a missionary herself, and a minister's wife for many years before she discovered that Jesus heals people today. Even healers develop.

The Gospels show—indeed, make a point—that Jesus' disciples often misunderstood him or even retreated from their faith. The best example is Peter's denial of Jesus after Jesus' arrest (Mark 14:66-72). Much of the time, though, it is just that the disciples' faith is still developing. Mark 4:10-13 shows that the disciples did not always understand Jesus' preaching and had to have the parables explained to them.

Why are there so many indications that the disciples' faith is incomplete? The Gospel writers want us to see this and determine not to make the same mistakes. One of the biggest mistakes that the disciples made occurs in the above story from Luke 5. The future disciples' first reaction to the miracle was to fear Jesus.

He has to calm them down before he can get on with calling them as disciples. Though it is always appropriate to be in awe of the Lord, it is not God's wish to strike fear into us. When we witness God's miracles, God does not want us to shrink away from him, but to come closer to him. Part of our development in faith should be renewed trust in God.

Why, then, do people not react positively to God's intervention? On both ends of the faith spectrum and in between, people often react first with fear, because God might just change their lives. I have known people who had a tremendous healing miracle in their lives, seemed to get scared of the very idea that God was that close, and went as far away from faith as they could get. Some people have that reaction to any close encounter with God.

There are several sources for people's fear. Sometimes they feel that with God around they are not going to be able to control their own lives anymore. Some have been brought up or taught to believe that God does not intervene. For these people, God's healing seems to threaten their whole worldview. Others have been raised with the idea that God is a terrible judge—a faulty picture of God—and thus they do not want the Lord close to them. Some people have had terrible childhood experiences with fathers who were absent or abusive. It is a terrible sorrow to me that these people cannot relate to the God whom I so fondly call "Father." (For these people, I suggest another way of addressing God, whatever is comfortable for them.)

Many people do not understand that what we are talking about is the power of God's love. The central model of God in the New Testament is "God is love. Whoever lives in love lives in God, and God in him. In this way, love is made complete among us so that we will have confidence on the day of judgment. . . . There is no fear in love. But perfect love drives out fear, because fear has to do with punishment. . . . We love because [God] first loved us" (1 John 4:16-19). Add to this "This is the message we have heard from him. . . . In him there is no darkness at all" (1 John 1:5). The full meaning of the cross and of all of God's other interventions in our life is to fill us with the power of God's love in this world and in the next. God's love will not make a puppet or a slave of us, making us do things we do not want to do. Rather, the experience of the Lord's love will give us more and more healthy control over the things for which we are responsible, including our life, faith, and work.

So there are two points to remember. First, everyone can develop in faith; and miracles are one of the Lord's resources for helping us do that. Second, one way or another, many people have been denied the spiritual or emotional ability to invite the Lord to come closer to them—let alone to intervene in their lives. However, the Lord can use even this to help people.

The most dramatic healing in which I ever had a part demonstrates clearly that very often desperation comes first, then God's response, and then a truly biblical faith. This couple had several of the reasons not to believe, which I just mentioned. They had never read the Bible and had little exposure to biblical faith. They were medical people, a physician and a nurse, whose medical education years ago had not disposed them to look for miracles. They did fear God taking control of their lives.

It happened that the physician's father had a particularly virulent form of cancer, with a prognosis of a long, slow, extremely painful death. There was nothing that could be done. What was worse, the father was in so much pain that he had to be held down by restraints on his arms and legs, and his oxygen mask was very tightly strapped to his face so that he could not pull it off by accident.

As medical professionals, the son and daughter-in-law knew all about this illness; also, they were not too sure about me, their new minister. Yet one day in June, the wife called me and asked, "How long are we going to have to go through this illness? How long before my father-in-law dies?"

At that point, the prognosis was seven or eight months. I knew nothing about medicine and was about to say something like, "God knows, be patient." However, out of my mouth came, "It will all be over by the end of the summer."

What had I said? I was flustered but could not improve the situation by taking back the words. I feel, and felt then, that the Lord had given me those words for them, but it still was intimidating to realize that they would look to me if I had made a mistake. Worse, before I could say anything more, she said thanks and hung up.

A short while later I preached the only sermon I had ever preached at that church about Jesus healing today. The son and daughter-in-law had come to church that Sunday, and afterward they invited me over so they could ask more about Jesus' healing. Desperate, they wanted to do something for the father. So we talked for a long time about the father, who had had a long, full life and had recently settled some previously unresolved issues.

The couple briefly mentioned that maybe they should pray for him to be taken. However, they also said that they really could not pray that prayer. It was just too hard emotionally to (effectively) say to God that the father should die. I said to them, "Why do you begrudge him his heavenly reward? Jesus earned it for him." They looked startled. They'd never thought about it that way.

We continued to talk until midnight. As I was about to leave, they said they thought maybe now they could pray for him to be taken to God, but they couldn't do it by themselves. Would I pray that for them before I left? They believed, but they needed help in their unbelief.

So I put one of them on either side of me on their couch, put an arm around each, and prayed. An image, a strong mind's-eye image, kept coming to me, and I just spoke the image I was "seeing." I pictured the father in a hospital bed. The restraints and the oxygen mask were fastened very tightly, and he was thrashing in pain and in total disarray. He was alone. Then, silently, Jesus walked into the room. Jesus removed the restraints and the oxygen mask. Jesus touched him and gave him one moment of total peace, joy, and freedom from pain on this earth. Then he spoke to the father and invited him to come along to another place where there is no more pain or weeping or suffering of any kind.

The father accepted. In peace and serenity, he left the room, and this earth, with Jesus.

I did not hear from the couple for another week. On August 7, I went into the church office and found a phone number on my desk. It had no name on it, and no one in the church knew who had put it there. But I had a hunch. It had an area code in another city and something within me strongly said I should call. So I did.

My physician parishioner answered the phone. He could not figure out how I'd gotten the phone number. He had had to leave town so quickly that he'd not had time to call me or to leave the number with anyone. The number I'd called was his parents', halfway across the country.

He told me his father had died the previous day, thus ending the illness well before the worst pain that is typical of that form of cancer. I asked whether he realized that his father had died on the Feast of the Transfiguration? Since the son was not familiar with that feast day, I explained that on that date much of the church celebrates Jesus' transformation before his disciples, when he shone as a heavenly being. On that occasion, God told the disciples that Jesus was God's own son. This, God said, is who Jesus really is—transfigured from the merely-earthly, into his true, heavenly appearance.

Absolutely amazed, my physician friend said he couldn't talk anymore, but he would tell me the whole story later. Actually, it was several months before he and his wife told me the whole story. A couple of days before the phone call, the father had been taken to the hospital. (Unknown to me, he had not been in the hospital when I'd prayed for him.) They had been told they should come, but the physician could not leave town right away. So the wife had gone first. She'd arrived at night and had gone straight to the hospital, where she found her father-in-law alone in his room. He was tied down by the restraints and his oxygen mask was on very tightly. His covers were terribly crumpled and wound together. He was unconscious or sleeping and clearly in terrible pain.

She could not stand to see him that way anymore. So she gathered up all of her courage, laid her hands on his head, and as nearly as she could remember it, she prayed for him the prayer that I had prayed in her living room.

The next morning, very early, she went back to the hospital. As before, the father-in-law was alone in his room, but he was sitting up. His eyes were open, and he was smiling, with a deeply peaceful look on his face. The restraints and the oxygen mask had been taken off and were neatly folded on the bed.

And he was dead.

She ran to find a nurse or doctor. No one knew that her father-in-law had died, nor did anyone know who had been with him when he died or who had removed the restraints. As a nurse, the daughter-in-law knew that when someone dies, the first thing medical professionals do is close the eyes. Next, they inform the attending physician. Neither had been done. No one had been there. She didn't know whether she was more afraid to find out that someone had been there or that they hadn't. It was so exactly like what she, her husband, and I had prayed for.

The next day her husband had come. He had had a migraine, which for him always lasted for days. But when his wife told him about the prayer, he thought perhaps prayer could work for him too. He prayed about his migraine, and it left instantly. Just at that moment, I had called. We never found out who left the phone number.

It doesn't really matter whether more people were involved than we knew. God had left his signature. The father had gone to his reward and left this life a happy man. And he had been transfigured, first in this life and then, as we believe, in the next.

These people had not had a clue that their own faith included this type of heavenly intervention. They were simply desperate and ready to ask God for whatever he could give them.

That is the requirement. All else, especially the final outcome, is and should be up to God. You pray and then your part is done. God will do whatever God will do. Father Mulcahy was wrong about only one thing: it is supposed to work that way.

Prayer Starter

If you can't pray for healing, pray for the ability to pray. Doing so is like saying, help my unbelief.

Or try praying something like this:

Lord, I want to believe, but I am more desperate and afraid than anything else. Help my faith. Please heal those things in my past and present that are keeping me distant from you. And please heal this illness. Thank you in advance for your intervention in our daily life and in this situation. Amen.

Chapter 5

A New Heart

This chapter pursues an important part of the "why not" question that we began to address in chapter 2. Even though some of the ways in which we keep God at a distance do not limit what the Lord is able to do, they do deprive us of the sense of God's love near to us. Let us begin with a story that is a good figure for this problem and its solution.

In January 1986, a fourteen-year-old girl named Donna Ashlock lay in a San Francisco hospital, dying of an enlarged heart. A fifteen-year-old boy named Felipe Garza was in the same hospital. He had headaches, but beyond that there was nothing seriously wrong with him, as far as anyone knew. Felipe had heard that Donna was also in the hospital. He knew her from school and admired her; they had even had one date. One day when his parents were visiting him, in an unguarded moment, and without any explanation, Felipe suddenly said, "If I die, give her my heart."

A few days later, Felipe had a stroke and he did, unexpectedly, die. His heart went to Donna, and it was a match—as unlikely as that is. "I've been born again" is how Donna described what happened. When a reporter asked her to explain what she meant, she replied, "I'm alive again. Felipe gave his heart to me." But then she looked sad and said, "He had to die to do it."

This story is a good figure for the message of salvation and also for the character of Jesus the healer. It is ultimately Jesus who died for us. Think about it this way: he gave his whole heart for us, physically and spiritually. And when he did that, he accomplished something nobody else had ever done—the spiritual part of salvation, the provision of our life after this life, with God.

There is another analogy here too. We need healing because, in biblical terms, we are all suffering from heart disease. Our particular heart disease is caused by continually failing love for God. No one is totally faithful to the Lord, no matter how much faith we have. Some of us actively keep the Lord away, knowingly or unknowingly. If any one problem opens us up for suffering, it is a lack of closeness to the Lord.

To understand this, we have to go back to the prophets. The "heart disease" of God's people is a big subject with them. (Look up "heart" in a Bible concordance and you will see that its listing takes up several pages.) Portraying God's people as God's bride who has been unfaithful, the prophets talk of the unfaithful heart: "I warned them again and again, saying 'Obey me.' But they did not listen or pay attention; instead, they followed the stubbornness of their evil hearts" (Jeremiah 11:7-8). "This is what the Lord says: 'Cursed is the one who trusts in man, who depends on flesh for his strength and whose heart turns away from the Lord'" (Jeremiah 17:5). The Lord accuses the people of having a heart of stone because they will not listen to the prophets and return to God.

The heart has a special place in the biblical concept of faithfulness. In our modern culture we think of it differently. We think of the heart as the seat of emotion. The Hebrews and various other ancient peoples thought of the emotions as being controlled in the belly. For them the heart was the seat of decision. They believed it was where commitments are made—specifically the commitment to be faithful to God. It was that commitment that was broken; that is why the people had heart disease.

But the prophets told us of a cure: God saw that people were not able to be faithful. Their hearts were not strong enough. Part of their heart disease was involuntary. They were born with it. So through the prophet Ezekiel, the Lord promised us all a heart transplant. Listen to this: "I will cleanse you from all your impurities. . . . I will give you a new heart and put a new spirit in you; I will remove from you your heart of stone and give you a heart of flesh. And I will put my Spirit in you. . . . You will be my people, and I will be your God" (Ezekiel 36:25-28).

God also pledged his heart to them. God would be faithful to them even though they were not faithful to him. Thus we are the recipients of God's heart in two ways: we get the heart transplant, the good one that does not fail, and we get God's faithful heart, always ready to love us.

But why do we need a heart transplant? The world as a whole has an imperfect commitment to God and has, ever since Eve and Adam, disobeyed the Lord. In chapter 3 we discussed how we are subject to the sin of the world and Jesus Christ is our only truly powerful defense against that. The young girl in the hospital is a good example of being subject to the sin of the world. She didn't do anything to deserve that enlarged heart, but she could have died from it. That is the sin of the world—the evil that is not our own personal fault. That is why we all need the spiritual heart transplant.

Heart disease can be fatal, so we need to make sure we have the right medicine at hand: the Lord in our hearts. Like any other medicine, it is very expensive. It cost Jesus his earthly life. For us, on one hand, it is free; on the other, it costs us our whole heart, our total commitment to the Lord. The great commandment tells us this. Jesus taught, "Love the Lord your God with all your heart and with all your soul and with all your mind" (Matthew 22:37, quoting Deuteronomy 6:5). Every way you can think of your heart, it must belong to God. No matter whether you can see the results, you put your trust in God. Part of this is allowing God into your situation for whatever God wants to do there—no matter what that is. Most of us are not called upon to give our physical heart, but the commitment we are asked to make is just that radical. It is a decision, and we have to make it for ourselves.

If you offer the Lord your heart, it will not be without result. The Lord told his people, through the prophet Jeremiah, "You will seek me and find me when you seek me with all your heart" (Jeremiah 29:13).

Emily was someone who had physical heart disease. I didn't know her, but I was a minister in a small city that had just one hospital and the nurses there knew all of the local ministers. Emily had had a massive heart attack, and her family had said she was of my denomination. Her minister could not be reached. Emily was likely to die at any moment.

Unaware of any of this, I had awakened at 2 a.m. Unable to figure out why, I decided to occupy myself by praying, thinking I would probably fall asleep in midprayer. But instead, an hour passed and I was still wide awake. So I asked the Lord what it was he might want of me. I felt a little like Samuel when he woke up at night, having heard the Lord call his name. Samuel asked God what he wanted, and God answered him. I thought, "What can it hurt?" So I asked.

Just then the phone rang. It was the hospital. They were afraid Emily was going to die without clergy attending. Could I come?

I was dressed in no time at all. As it happened, I had almost no gas in the car and no wine in the communion kit. I could not believe I had let my two most important "vehicles" run empty, but it was too late now. God would have to take care of it. There was no time, and anyway, nothing in that town was open at that hour. How I got to the hospital I do not know, except that I prayed for the Lord to take me and my car the five miles or so to the hospital and I would worry about getting home later.

Emily's family was gathered at the hospital. When I arrived, one of them said, "Whatever you do, don't do last rites. You'll scare her to death." ("Aha!" I thought, "I won't need the communion kit." Emily was unconscious and could not have taken bread or wine anyway.) I asked, "What about a healing service? Even death can be a healing, especially a godly death."

They latched onto that. "Yes, a healing service."

I stood next to Emily's bed. She looked ashen, as if she were dead already. I looked up to find the family and the entire staff of the cardiac care unit crowding into her cubicle and overflowing into the hall. I prayed for healing. Moved to tears by her situation, I bent down and kissed her on the forehead, and then I left.

The next morning I went back to Emily's room. I expected to find that Emily had died, as everyone had said she would. But not knowing any other place to go to contact the family, I decided I would start there.

When I got to her room, I found that Emily was still alive. When I asked whether the doctor expected her to die that morning, the nurse looked at me oddly, paused, and then replied, "Uh, I don't know. Are—are you going to pray for her again?"

"Of course. Why?"

"Last night, when you prayed for healing, her vitals came back. She just might be OK."

I prayed for Emily again.

After that, for two weeks I visited her and prayed for her and talked with her. I found out that her husband had had an accident at work and his company was giving him a hard time about paying him either his salary or a disability check. They could not seem to resolve the matter, so the husband was actually bringing in no money at all—on top of having medical bills. This had been going on for many weeks, and Emily had taken it on herself to "fix" things. Not that there was anything she could actually do to change the situation. But evidently she was the family worrier. Most families have one of those. Such a person takes on the whole emotional burden of whatever hurts the rest of the family. Worriers feel that if they do not carry the problem around inside of them, something will go wrong that could have been avoided. It is as if the worriers have stationed themselves at the guardhouse and are determined to be vigilant at all cost. Emily had done just this. She also had literally worried herself into a massive heart attack.

Even in the hospital, she was worried about her husband. She talked continually about his situation, and anytime I tried to talk with her about taking care of herself, the subject returned to him. This is typical of the family worrier, but in this case, it had an obsessive ring to it, and that really troubled me.

I tried and tried to tell her she'd have to let go. I was seriously worried that if she did not stop dwelling on the disability problem, she would have another heart attack. We talked about letting God handle both the disability and the heart attack. She saw the point, but she said, "I can't let go. I can't feel good about any of it. I just can't."

I explained I was not saying she should feel good about it. I was saying let God handle it. "It's a decision you make," I said. "A decision." For quite a while I could not get off of that word "decision." I feared I was beginning to be a source of stress myself, but I felt compelled to repeat the word once more. "I'll think about it," she said.

Even though half of her heart had been destroyed, she was soon well enough to be moved to another hospital. Then a week later, the phone rang again. Emily's family had been called to the hospital. Would I go along?

There we were greeted by a nurse who only shook her head. No words. We knew Emily had died. The family wanted the last rites this time. Family and nursing staff—in contrast to that last late-night visit—left me starkly alone in Emily's room. It seemed they wanted and needed to stay as far from death as they could— yet they felt a heart-wrenching responsibility and desire to take care of Emily in regard to spiritual things. It was very hard to be in that room looking at her very still, darkly gray face. I read the prescribed prayers with some difficulty.

When I came out, I asked the nurse, "Can you tell us anything? What happened?" The nurse described how Emily had been making a remarkable recovery. Especially that day. "Today she was really happy for the first time," the nurse said. "She was happy all day and seemed to have relaxed. And she kept saying she had made a decision. She had made a decision. She had made a decision. She just kept saying that."

And then she was dead—quietly, peacefully, suddenly, gone.

That was when I knew. I already knew that a significant contributing factor in her heart attack had been that she had been so deeply stressed. In effect, she had tried to be God. She had tried to be the guardian for her husband, the impossible situation, and the family's well-being. But the situation was one of those things that is fallout from the sin of the world—something undeserved, not solvable by human means. In effect, unknowingly she had tried to take on this effect of the sin of the world all by herself. She had helped to make herself sick—ironically, because she loved her family. But the healthy way to love the family was to love and trust God first. Let the Lord resolve the situation, and trust him to do it.

I well understood what decision she had made. She had given her whole heart to God, and with it, the family and their care. She no longer had to resolve the problem by herself. And with that, she was free. She had been given new life for long enough to resolve her own issues and to be at peace.

There's more. In her decision, I think she accomplished a real miracle, maybe two. Shortly after her decision and her death, the disability claim was settled and things became much more peaceful for her husband. Any time a person makes a genuine commitment to the Lord, the Lord is given a straight, clear avenue into the situation. Emily's decision committed the future progress of her and her husband's life to the Lord. Her decision had invited the Lord into the situation. The timing of the legal and financial resolution was a coincidence—but one of those that seems to be stamped with the Lord's own signature.

Her situation also had impacted someone else. Four months later, after I had taken a church in another state, I received a letter from a nurse in the hospital where I had done the healing service. In the envelope was a page out of the local newspaper on which there was a public relations advertisement. "Get to know your local hospital employees," it said. "Employee of the month . . . ," and it had a picture of a young man. The nurse wrote, "I was there the night you did the healing service for Emily. We all were, including the man in this photo. He is a nurse and up until that night he drove us all crazy with extremely bitter and cynical talk. He talked and talked about how God doesn't care about us and about what a fake the church is. And he would never let up. But when he saw the healing service and saw how Emily's vitals snapped back, he shut up. It's been four months, and he has never said another cynical word. He's going to a church in town now."

Any genuine spiritual healing is going to have constructive effects beyond the one healed, even if someone dies in the process. Emily and her initial healing had effectively healed someone else's spiritual heart disease. This was another sign to me that her later death was a resolution, a godly conclusion, rather than a tragedy. And seeking God with all of her heart, I am sure that Emily surely did find him.

Prayer Starter

Don't try to be God by taking control of the impossible situation. Give God credit for being God and being able to handle it, and then give God free reign within your situation, to do whatever is right. Try this:

> *Lord, I give you my whole heart. Please use all of me to bring healing into this situation. Thank you and bless you for whatever you choose to do. Amen.*

This is not an easy assignment. No one can make it possible for you to say this prayer and mean it, or mean it and also get some visible result. It took Emily—in her extreme situation of need—quite a long time to come to the point where she had a sense of resolution and release. The point is to say these words in regard to some situation of your own or someone else's, let them stir within your spirit for a while, and say them again. Just the effort will begin to work a change in you, and whether or not you see the "answer," you will have offered your whole heart to the Lord.

Chapter 6

Bridging the Gap

Often the greatest problem in asking for healing, even for people of faith, is the sense that we have no control over the situation and, above all, no control over whether God will act. This chapter addresses that problem, and it begins with a figure for Christians who find themselves "in the breach."

Recently, I saw a greeting card with a picture of two trapeze artists, both high up in the air. One was suspended by his toes from a swing. His entire body and his arms were stretched out toward the other trapeze artist, who had taken the critical leap. The leaping artist was suspended in midair, in the big gap between the swing he had left and his partner's outstretched arms. With no net below, he was entirely dependent upon the one who still had hold of a swing. Far below were hundreds of pinpoint-sized heads, looking up wondering what would happen next. Would the trapeze artist fall? Would he be saved by the one with the connection above? The crowd, too, was suspended, between wonder and fear, hope and helplessness.

Inside the card was the message "Thanks for being there."

This card is a metaphor for our relationship with Jesus Christ. It is also a metaphor for the gap between our everyday, practical life and the spiritual connection we must make if we are going to experience spiritual healing.

God sent Jesus to bridge that critical gap between the world and heaven, between the effects of sin and real spiritual well-being. As Paul writes in Romans 7, we cannot help ourselves. We are subject both to sin and to the effects of the sin of the world, which, as we have noted, include illness and death. In despair, Paul writes, "What a wretched man I am! Who will rescue me from this body of death?" But then he goes on, "Thanks be to God—through Jesus Christ our Lord!" (Romans 7:24-25). In other words, "Thank you, God, for being there for us, through Jesus." Jesus has a special connection to heaven, the life-saving, all-important tie to God. He had to leap into the breach to be there for us. But in so doing, he provided us with the one link we needed to be saved from illness and death, spiritually and physically. The Letter of First John puts it this way: "This is love: not that we loved God, but that he loved us and sent his son" to save us (1 John 4:10).

Another element in the picture is our response. We have to take the critical leap with conviction and then trust God to catch us. In the greeting card picture of the leap, there is an invisible force at work that has highly visible results: momentum, which carries the suspended man all the way across the gap into the arms of the other in whom he has put his trust. For Christians, that force is the power of the Holy Spirit.

We need the power of the Spirit in our lives. Like the picture of the trapeze artist, frozen in time as it is, all of our life is lived in the breach. Christians are aware that this breach is the gap between the first coming and the second, between our initial faith and our own realization of the resurrection, between the sickness of the world and the salve of the Holy Spirit. There is always a gap that is, by solely human power, unbreachable. To get from one side to the other, we need to claim and invoke by prayer the power of the Holy Spirit. We need this whether the issue is just living day-to-day in a stressful job or getting from real illness to wholeness in mind, body, or spirit.

One more thing about the card: the moment depicted is the most uncertain, the most frightening. One of the most important points for Christians to learn is this: the "save" is always in the most frightening part of the drama. It is the part when we are truly suspended with no net. We recognize this when we are desperate for some type of healing. Most often, all we see is the breach and how far we are apparently about to fall. We have no idea, in this situation, how to help ourselves. Thus it is important to remind ourselves—even if we cannot quite believe it—that God is in charge of the outcome.

The following is an extreme but true example showing just how dark things can be before the Lord steps in. The apparent hopelessness of a situation is not an indication of whether the Lord will act. In a sense, such darkness and hopelessness is turned to God's glory, because the Lord's intervention shines so much more brightly against such a backdrop.

It is important to understand that I do not record these experiences with any lack of forgiveness. I want to tell you about a particular church because since this experience I have lived with both a power of wonder at what the Lord can do and a love for people that I would never have been able to have before. This inner transformation came about because I now know that the Lord is my defense and my chief resource, and with him I can go through anything. I live to see the glory of God again. But even if I never do, this one experience has shown me that the Lord is always really there.

I had just gone to the first church in which I was the senior pastor and there instantly found myself very much in the breach, with no net. When I arrived, I found waiting for me the previous month's newsletter, in which the search committee apologized on the front page for having hired a woman. I also found a formal letter, typed and signed, from the man who turned out to have the only sizable pledge. It declared that he was not coming to church again till I was gone. Later I found out that this was because the people—and this man in particular—felt I had been imposed upon them by the diocese. This was, in some part, true. The diocese had been desperate. No one else would take this troubled and desperately poor parish. I had taken it out of a sense of serving where I was most needed and because I absolutely had to find a job. Coming from another state, I did not know about the church's problems other than the general lack of money that is common to so many parishes.

I set out to do my job. When they get to know me, they will see that I really do care about them, I figured, and the only way for that to happen was for me to be with them. Yet I began to hear rumors that I never did any work. It seemed my job and career might easily be jeopardized by such idle talk.

I also learned there was real illness of a sort among the people of the parish. The parish had been founded in an atmosphere of bitterness and dissent, and those emotions had lingered. A bigger parish had founded this small one, but half the members of the large parish had felt that their parish's attendance would be harmed by the new church. The resulting ill will had been so strong that the other half had to have the organizing meeting in a building belonging to another denomination. Twenty years later, all of the founding members were still around and the contrary atmosphere persisted.

The last three pastors had all been somehow disabled on the job. One had been fired. Another had had heart disease that got so much worse after he arrived that he had been confined to the rectory. (I came to know this man, who had become miraculously healthy since leaving the parish.) The third had succumbed to a clinical depression and had stayed either at home or at the home of one parishioner for three years.

At first I thought, poor ministers; it's a tough job. Then I began to understand that the bitter atmosphere in that parish had disabled all three of them. In many small parishes, the pastor is a sort of locus where people take out their frustrations with God. In a healthier situation, that would have been lost among many positive aspects of the relationship. Instead two or three laypeople wanted to have control of that parish, and they were not going to let anyone else in on it. No one wanted to confront or openly contradict them.

Those two or three people had been the "disablers." They exerted so much pressure of all kinds that the previous ministers had not been able to do anything for their church. Thus in more than a decade, nobody at that church had had any experience of a pastor who did anything pastoral. There also had been no Bible teaching by anyone who was trained in the Bible. The church had become a place for mostly social gathering rather than shared religious activity.

In this parish, their way of being a church was not meanness, but rather a terrible hunger, the kind that makes you feel raw inside. This hunger became abundantly clear one day when after months of insisting that we get out of services by noon "because the children must have their lunch," the parishioners asked if we could have Bible study right after church. They hired a babysitter for the kids, and every person who had come to church stayed for an hour.

They began to have a taste of the riches of Scripture, starting with the Gospel of John. Around that time, the people's pledges began to go up. However, there was still so much friction from the two or three disablers—who had decided to stay away—that I felt that my job was in more jeopardy than ever. Despite my true gratification that we were filling a hunger, I did not think that I was going to make it to the next job without a mental or physical breakdown of some sort. Clearly, this parish needed healing— healing of their past and its residue of bitterness, healing of their relationships with one another, and healing of many long-standing individual hurts and illnesses that I was beginning to glimpse.

I decided to pray every day for the two or three disablers, in particular the man who had written the letter. I also decided absolutely not to try to engineer a human solution. The situation was too volatile. So I did, every single day, pray for healing for them all, and for that one man especially.

In addition to the difficulties that were inherent in the job, I had a life-long embarrassment that made me more vulnerable and open to criticism. Since I was eleven years old, my skin had never behaved. I had gone to doctors, but there was no human help for my problem. I had prayed and prayed about it for twenty-five years, but to that point, I had had only one answer, an insight that the skin problems were the result of family stress and that in a sense I was beating myself up from inside. Hence the welts on the outside. I tried to ignore the problem, but I wanted to know how to make that special connection to God that would heal me.

Some months before I went to this new church, my counselor had laid hands on my face and prayed for healing. I had felt powerfully within myself at the time that a healing was occurring, and I do feel that there was a direct connection with the healing I was to have. However, it was not until all of these months later that I saw the result, significantly while trying to find a way toward healing for others (the people of this church). The delay (or God's timing) of my healing made me all the more eager to know how to bridge the critical gap between me and God for their sake as well as my own.

I tried to occupy myself with something positive in my job and thus decided to borrow a pile of books about Christian spiritual healing. My mother had always prayed for people's healing, and for her, it seemed to work. Other than reading my counselor's own book, *The Case for Spiritual Healing,* I had never read any modern books about healing. Thus I had never been exposed to the experience of many of the great people in healing ministry. I wanted to know all I could about healing; maybe my reading would yield some guidance about healing this parish. In the meantime, I also found great comfort in the accounts of God helping people.

I read and read, and through it all, I had one question. These books were largely about healing in the context of large groups of people, as at healing conferences. It's one thing to pray for myself, I thought. God and I go way back, as they say, and I had a sense of connection there—even if I did not always receive the prayed-for healing. But what about praying for other people? What about doing it as part of the church's program, in the name of the church—which it would be, since I was there in the capacity of the ordained? I felt as if there was a critical gap between me-and-God, on one hand, and these people, on the other. First, there was the bad relationship that seemed to come with the job. There was also the whole consideration of what if I did pray for healing for them and healing did not occur? How should I look at that? Finally, there was the most obvious gap: getting the parish to allow me to pray for healing for them. The gaps I felt between me and actually bringing healing to these people were too many and too great for me to fix.

The single most important thing about the gaps is that our own limitations simply do not define what the Lord can do. We do not really need to do anything. The Lord can and does simply step in to change a bad situation.

I kept reading. As it happened, I was at home. I went into the bathroom and out of the corner of my eye something in the mirror seemed different. I thought, no, it's the power of suggestion. I had thought maybe my skin had started to clear up a bit. I read some more. A couple of hours later I went by a mirror again. This time there was an unmistakable difference. After that, I read and read till I got to the bottom of that pile of books on healing. Every couple of hours, I looked in the mirror. My face changed before my eyes. I was healed; the condition has never come back in the twelve years since.

Did the reading clear up my skin? Well, yes, in a way. I began to feel more and more confident in God's intervention as I read, and gradually throughout the reading, a soft cloud of the Holy Spirit seemed to descend upon me and my situation. I was truly transported, as one is, for example, after singing praise songs for a couple of hours. That is the way I felt; my mood had changed from despair to praise, and I knew that the Lord was personally present with me. Of course, he did the healing. I had asked for healing during my counselor's prayer, but the Lord used the books as a shoe horn to put me into a spiritual place where I could receive the healing.

Something else had happened. Through the healing of my skin, I had seen how the gap was to be bridged. The answer was: not by me. My years of prayer and scripture study had not hurt. In fact, I am sure they helped me come to this point. But the thing I had never before grasped was this: I have no control over actually bridging the gap or over when or how it occurs—and thank God. Because it is God's job. I had just seen how effective God was at that, too. No wonder Paul virtually shouts, "Thank God for bridging the gap through Jesus Christ!"

Throughout the reading, of course, I had prayed and thought about how healing could be brought to the people of this church. But again, I was not to be the agent of change. Some days later I went to the next parish meeting, afraid, as usual, of what was going to come my way this time. To my drop-jawed astonishment, the people said, in consensus, "Kamila, we need something. This parish is really hurting. Isn't there something you can do? Like—maybe—a healing service?"

What? A healing service? Yes, a healing service. They voted to hold a healing service as the main service the first Sunday of the next month. Was their request—following upon my reading of the books on healing—just a coincidence? Yes, of course. That is one way of knowing that it is God, not me, who brought about this magnificent change.

There is more—a lot more—to this story, including many physical and spiritual healings that occurred at the healing services that were to follow. The situation of the man who had written the letter had a resolution, too, though it would take much too long to explain it here. However, the main thing is I was permanently changed by that experience. I knew that God had been there with me and I was ready to let go of a lot of things I had felt I had to control—besides my job.

I also had seen a critical aspect of my life with God that had never been clear. I realized that in my family life and my church life, and in some sense of which I had not been aware, in my faith, I had always felt like a flying trapeze artist, with no swing of my own and no net. That is a picture of stress. But a force I had not been able to see had healed me and begun to heal other people using me. I came to see that that lack of control was a good thing. I could trust the Lord who is in control.

The healing I experienced there also propelled me to a new place in my life and in my career. Soon afterward I was invited to another parish where they never gave me a hard time and where they openly appreciated everything and anything I did for them. That new parish adopted healing as their statement of parish purpose.

What I said then, and what I still say, about all of it is "Thank you, God, for being there."

Prayer Starter

Read the Bible a little bit every day. Thank God for it. This rhythm alone will start, or continue, your swing in tandem with the Lord and make you more available for the work of the Holy Spirit. Pray something similar to this prayer:

I need this impossible problem to be healed. I acknowledge that I don't have control over it, but you do. Take control, then, and propel me into your own arms for whatever healing, comfort, and resolution you have in store for me. Thank you, God, for being there. Amen.

Chapter 7

Finding the Father in Heaven

M any of us simply do not know the keenness with which small children feel something like death. We also tend to be unaware of the profundity of their spiritual experiences. So we do not explain things to them, and we do not try to elicit from them their own experience. We think that because children have few words, they have little knowledge and shallow experience.

That is not true. My first experience of transcendence and of the Father in heaven came when I was a young girl. The experience began with grief and a healing and burgeoned into a concrete, personal version of what is really the whole quest of the people of God: in the words of Jeremiah, "You will seek me [God] and find me when you seek me with all your heart" (Jeremiah 29:13).

My grandfather was called "Tatí," a Czech word that means "Dad" but is used as a fond form of address. It means more than "daddy," though, and any generation might address my grandfather in that way. He was the father of the generations. His language was Czech, and while he was alive that was the language of the household. My first word had been a Czech word pronounced "Dyedek," another fond name for grandfather. But just between the time when I was learning to recognize words and the time when I began to speak, Tatí died, and the language of the household switched to English.

My grandfather died when I was three and a half, but no one told me he had died or explained his absence to me. No one explained anything. All I knew was the magic had gone. I would hold onto my mother, saying "Mama, Mama," but she didn't seem to know I was there. A dark thing seemed to have wrapped her up. She looked down and her hands hid her face. I could not get through to her. I was scared because she had always focused on me; I was important. But I wasn't now. In my child's mind, this empty experience went on forever.

Another day, and there was an odd quiet in the house. My grandfather still was not there. Somehow I knew he was not in the house at all. He wasn't in the garden he had kept so carefully, and he wasn't out for a walk. Somehow I knew. No one mentioned him. That was how I knew. He wasn't coming. Where could he be? I had to know. Yet I couldn't know.

I would find him myself. I could do it. So I looked. But I didn't disturb the quiet.

I looked in his room. It was quiet. I looked in his closet. His big leather jacket hung in there. The whole closet smelled warm and fragrant, like Tatí. But he was, of course, not there.

One afternoon I had given up on the closets and set to walking from room to room. I walked into the dining room. On either end, there was a stuffed chair. The nearer one was his, the chair where my grandfather had sat with me on his lap and told me stories. I didn't remember any of the stories, but I remembered his scent, his warm lap and chest, and his arms around me. And I remembered how he loved to sit in that chair.

As I passed his chair, I looked—and there he was. Just as usual. I knew it. I had found him.

He spoke to me, with his glorious, rich voice. His voice was so familiar and so stirring down inside of me. For two or three minutes he spoke to me most earnestly in Czech. I couldn't understand. I did recognize common phrases of his by their sound, but I didn't know what he was saying. Also, without explanation, I smelled roses.

I couldn't contain myself. I was torn between staying with him and getting my mother. I called and called to her. Finally, I yanked myself out of Tatí's presence, willing him to be there when I came back, and went to get Mama. But when we got back to his chair, it was empty.

Always after that she would say, "I knew you were seeing something. You were so excited. I just couldn't understand what you were trying to say." When she finally did understand that it was Tatí, she never doubted me. I never doubted. I don't doubt it to this day. He was there, just as if in the flesh. And he spoke to me, telling me something I had to know. Something I, as a baby, could not repeat and did not fully understand. All I knew was, I had reached, I had found him, and I had been given something of immense importance—him. He had never left me.

From this one experience, I remembered Tatí's face, accurately, until I was in my twenties. Then one day we all went to the family cemetery and I recognized his picture there solely from my vision of him. Many years after his visit, I would, every once in a while for no reason, smell roses in the middle of winter in our closed-up house, with no flowers in sight. I would recognize that as the scent of the experience and know that it had been real.

Thus began a decades-long part of my life, a part of my life that was so important that it formed everything I did. It had a title: "Searching for the Father." My first attempt had been a success, though it was clear that this was only because he had wanted to be found. The origin of this experience was probably in my missing my own absent father, but the end result was something magnificent. I was later to search again, in another time of bereavement, a figurative but real bereavement when I was twelve and thirteen. And that time I found the Father in heaven. And since then, I have never lost him.

I believe the reason I was able to start early toward a genuine and personal religious faith was because, left in a vacuum that had to be filled, I had searched and searched, against what were humanly impossible circumstances. I had begun this search because I had a child's innocence and imagination. I was not yet too educated to think my search foolish, and I have kept the knowledge I found out so concretely through that vision: "If you seek me with all you heart, you shall surely find me." I had found not just Tatí, but the one I came to think of as my Grand Father in heaven. I had found transcendence. That meant that there were secrets to life that preserved its magic and its warmth and that would always be with me. I had also been healed of the empty, dull, too-quiet house that had been myself after the loss of my grandfather.

This must have been the way the disciples felt after the crucifixion, the first time they saw the risen Jesus. There they were, feeling bereft and without any idea what to do except to hide and huddle together. They were just like children, having lost their father and guide, their source of warmth and love and healing. Then all of a sudden, there he was. He showed them the wounds in his hands and his side, and he ate with them, the very same food they were eating. They knew it was Jesus, the same one, the source of love and hope and healing in their lives—and yet he had become transcendent. He could walk through locked doors and ascend into the presence of the Father in heaven, right before their eyes. They were thus healed of their grief at his earthly death.

More, they were filled with a hunger for the presence of the Lord. As Acts 1–2 shows, the disciples obeyed Jesus' command to wait for the gift of the Holy Spirit. When the Spirit came, they were filled with great spiritual riches and spent the rest of their lives serving the Lord and seeking him by awaiting his glorious return.

We often do not dwell on the resurrection appearances of Jesus as the healing of bereavement, but they are that. They are also so much more, of course. They are an invitation for us to seek the living Jesus in our own lives and to go to him for the healing of our griefs and hurts.

I knew another person who, as a small child, had a spiritual healing from grief and an introduction to the transcendent, just as I had had. He never stopped seeking and serving the Lord after that, either. An older, retired man in one of my parishes, he was one of the gentlest spirits I had ever known, and he was always ready with an offer of help or service of some kind.

One evening at a parish business meeting, he interrupted the proceedings to tell us his story. His mother had died when he was about four years old. He had been terribly lonely for her, and he had ached and ached to be cuddled in her arms again. After some time his father had remarried, a German woman (as he put it). She took care of him competently but always very matter-of-factly. There was no cuddling, no affection, no place for him to sink his grief or to assuage it.

One night he was lying in his bed, when all of a sudden, he saw a vision of his mother. She told him that everything was going to be all right. Then she was gone.

After that moment, his grief was healed. He never felt that terrible emptiness again. He had found his mother in heaven—and, as was evident from his adult behavior—also his Mother in heaven. After that, he also had managed to get along nicely enough with his stepmother. And that was why he always tried to help and comfort everyone else who needed it.

I have known many people who were deprived of an important source of love, either in childhood or in a time of life crisis. Many of these people became bitter or inflexible in the way they dealt with others. If you are one of these people, it is easy to say, "Well, I didn't get a vision. I guess God didn't care about me." There is an answer for you, in that case. God allowed such a moment of grief and loneliness to happen even to Jesus. It was at that moment on the cross when Jesus felt so deeply abandoned by his Father in heaven that he cried out, "My God, my God, why have you forsaken me?" (Matthew 27:46). Of course, God did answer him, by raising him up in the resurrection. But in the meantime, Jesus had all of the fear and grief we experience when we lose one of the anchors of our lives. Jesus handled grieving, loneliness, and desperate emptiness by confronting God directly with his complaint. That is not wrong for us, any more than it was wrong for Jesus.

The object is at least to hold on to the intellectual knowledge—the promise in Scripture—that God is hearing our utmost grief and that he is going to answer it. Perhaps it will not be with a vision, but certainly it will be with his own presence. We, after the resurrection, are never really alone. Jesus promised, "Surely I am with you always, to the very end of the age" (Matthew 28:20). You are not alone. Your Father in heaven has not forgotten you. Pray and seek for God, and just see what he will do.

Prayer Starter

Read Mark 14:32-36. If there is an area of desperation in your life, imagine yourself kneeling next to Jesus in the garden of Gethsemane when he is facing death. Try this model of healing prayer by praying verse 36 with him:

Abba, Father, everything is possible for you. Take this cup from me. Yet not what I will, but what you will. Amen.

Notice that:

1. Jesus addresses God as "Abba, Father." We know that Jesus senses God to be very close because Abba is also the Aramaic word for an ordinary father. It is probably the way the child Jesus addressed Joseph.

2. Jesus acknowledges his own hopelessness and prays from the midst of it.

3. He acknowledges God as the source of all hope ("everything is possible for you").

4. He then asks for what he needs in specific terms; "this cup" unquestionably refers to a specific state of and reason for his desperation—his coming death.

5. Then Jesus gives everything over to God, no matter what the outcome.

This is a perfect model for healing prayer. Try it. Pray about whatever loss seems hopeless in your life—whether it is the loss of a loved one or the loss of some thing.

Chapter 8

The Place of Praise in Healing

S ometimes the most effective route to healing or restoration is simply to praise God. As Psalm 22:3 puts it, the Lord dwells in the praises of Israel. (That is the way it reads in Hebrew, contrary to some English translations.) The Lord comes to dwell in some special way wherever God is praised. Did you know that the Hebrew word for "prayer"—generic prayer—actually means "praise"? The original, Hebrew worshipers of God did not think of prayer apart from praise.

Many people say, "But I can't praise God; I'm too miserable." I even heard one person mutter, "Why bother? God knows how great he is." If you don't feel good enough to praise God spontaneously or if praise does not feel comfortable to you, remember this: your use of it has to be sincere, but you don't have to like it. This is not a contradiction. We do lots of things out of obligation rather than out of feeling—like going to work and doing a good job because it is the right thing to do. Praise is sometimes hard for people if it is unfamiliar to them, and much of the time when we most need God we do not feel so good. However, many of the psalms and other texts of the Bible actually command us to praise God. They do so for good reasons; praise is a way of coming much closer to God, and God asks us to do it. It is, first of all, an obligation, but also the source of great benefit to us.

Once I was in a horribly bad mood because of an injustice by a good friend. I simply could not get the misunderstanding and anger between us to stop cascading, no matter what I tried. On top of that, I was stuck at the mechanic's, waiting for my car, never a pleasant task. Out of desperation at being stuck in two ways at once, I started to praise God. But it wasn't the way you probably think praise ought to sound. I was saying, "I'm in a really bad mood. I don't even want to feel better, and I don't think this will do any good. But anyway, praise you, Lord . . ." Every once in a while that day I said the same thing.

The next morning I woke up early and felt entirely different—not just about the misunderstanding, but about myself. What is more, I felt inspired to write. I got up and started working on my computer—which led to the discovery of a pleasant e-mail from my friend, one that let me know that the misunderstanding had been put to an end.

This type of thing happened to the Old Testament Israelites, too, only on a grander scale. They were under attack by the Ammonites and the Moabites, their traditional enemies, and there was no hope. Look at the order in which things happened to deliver the Israelites and the place of praise in that order. First, they receive the report: "A vast army is coming against you" (2 Chronicles 20:2). In response, Jehoshaphat, king of Judah, speaks to the Lord in front of the Israelites. "O Lord," he says, "you rule over all the kingdoms of the nations. Power and might are in your hand, and no one can withstand you" (20:6). Acknowledging God's greatness is a central aspect of praising him. Notice that praise is what Jehoshaphat does before even making a request. The praise part of Jehoshaphat 's prayer goes on for four long verses.

Only then does Jehoshaphat give voice to his people's complaint and request (20:10-12). Notice the utter despair in the words—despair even though, in his head, Jehoshaphat knows the power of the Lord and had just acknowledged it: "We have no power to face this vast army that is attacking us. We do not know what to do." Even his conclusion is not without pathos, and we can almost see the combination of hope and fear on his face: "But our eyes are upon you."

The Lord answers, "Do not be afraid or discouraged because of this vast army. For the battle is not yours, but God's" (20:15). He further promises that if the Israelites trust him and go toward the enemy, the Lord will win the battle. Before any of the promise was kept, while they were only setting out for the place where the enemy was, Jehoshaphat appointed people to sing, "Give thanks to the Lord, for his love endures forever." Then "as they began to sing and praise, the Lord set ambushes against the men . . . who were invading Judah, and they were defeated" (20:21-22). They did not even have to meet the enemy. It was as they were praising God that the victory was won, and that is not a coincidence. Praise came first, then God's promise; in the latter part of the story, praise was offered, and then help came. The praise came from the midst of darkness and hopelessness for the sake of obedience—not because they felt good at the time.

Praise is also integral to the New Testament story of the birth of the church. Acts 2 says that it was when the apostles were praising God that the Lord added to their numbers, that is, to the number of people who believed in Jesus. Praise is an essential part of worship in both testaments. There is a sense in which praising God is our whole purpose. According to 1 Peter 2:9, "You are a chosen people, a royal priesthood, a holy nation, a people belonging to God, that you may declare the praises of him who called you out of darkness." Hebrews 13:15 says, "Through Jesus, therefore, let us continually offer to God a sacrifice of praise—the fruit of lips that confess his name."

As the people of God, praise is our job description. These latter passages were written when the church as we know it today was just beginning. Believers were defining themselves as the church, and this is the way they did it. The assignment is not just believing in God, but active believing. Active believing is acting on our faith in the midst of the difficulties of life and even under duress, praising God at such times just because we are asked to do so. Active believing is not only celebrating the good things God has done for us in the past, but also helping to create healing outcomes. Active believing defies evil and misery by celebrating God from the very midst of darkness. Praise is one of our chief engines of active belief.

Two things go on when we praise God. One is on the simply human level. When we praise God—as Jehoshaphat did—our eyes are looking out over and above human and earthly things. We have set our heart of hearts upon God rather than on what troubles us. Therefore our vision is no longer limited to the human realm of possibility. The second thing is that we have called God into the situation, into our own lives and circumstances—something only we can do. The Lord will honor our invitation. Yes, he is everywhere already. Nevertheless, he wants our permission to intervene in our lives, and there is some sense in which he is in that situation with us when we invite him. When we do it with praise, we are also engaging in a unique form of positive thinking. Most importantly, we are honoring God in a way that is very special to him.

In praying for healing, we have to remember those principles. When we praise God from within a bad situation, we grant God dominion over that part of our lives that needs healing. We also look evil and illness in the face and defy them in a constructive and holy way.

There is one more step. Romans 8:28 says, "In all things God works for the good of those who love him." Some people say that this verse means it is "good" for us to suffer. That is not a biblical principle, and you should never believe that it is. If God wanted us to suffer, Jesus would never have healed people in the first place. Romans 8:28 does mean this: God can use everything for good for you. God will do some good with whatever you are going through, but it is because he cannot stand your suffering and wants with all of his heart to relieve it. Further, he intends to redeem your misery by creating an outcome that is healing. Even the worst thing in your life can be turned into good. God is good, and it is in God's nature to do this for you.

So, here is the "advanced lesson": praise God not only in the bad situation, but for it. This is not intuitive. It goes against the grain. But you are doing it for one very important reason. You have the opportunity to thank God in advance for the good he can make for you out of even the worst situation. That really is faith. It is also a powerful form of positive imaging. As Norman Vincent Peale spent his life teaching, positive thinking is itself an engine for creating a beneficial outcome.

Therefore, if it is necessary in order to get your praise going, tell God that you do not feel like praising. That kind of honesty can create a clearer "phone line" between you and God, and the praise will still "take."

One more principle will bring us to an illustration of the effects of praise. The good effects of any genuine healing should cascade. Praise also cascades, and combining it with healing prayer can have unhoped-for results.

The secretary in one of my churches belonged to a singing group that was based in her own Catholic parish. She offered to bring the group to sing while I was praying for people during the first of a new series of healing services. Our parishioners loved the music so much and loved being prayed for so much that the group had to sing everything they knew twice. People did receive healing at that service, although it did not become apparent until later. The more immediate result was that both the parishioners and the singing group went out and talked about the healing service and about the things God had done for them. The musical praising resulted in more people giving praise to God.

Shortly after that service, the secretary said she had a Catholic friend who needed prayer. Would I make a sort of house call? I went and found out that this unfortunate woman had had a partial colostomy, but the operation had not worked. She had been left wearing one of those terribly uncomfortable bags. What is still worse, she had had the operation a second time with the same result. She was now scheduled for a third operation, but she just couldn't face the possibility of another failure. The surgeries and the intervening times had been so painful and frustrating. She wanted me to pray about the third operation, which was coming up in just a few days.

Several of her children—all grown or teenagers—were at the house while I was there. I had known for a long time about the power of praise, but it was unusual for me to recommend only praise. However, this time, after talking with her, it just felt right. I told the woman to praise God as continuously as possible until the time for the surgery. She was sitting uncomfortably in her stuffed chair, looking so miserable. But she said, "OK," and I knew that she meant it. I told her children, standing around her chair, that until the operation their assignment was to praise God on their mother's behalf. They also agreed. For them, it seemed like something they could do about the situation.

About three weeks later, my secretary asked if I'd heard what happened to this woman, and when I said "No," she told me. The moment for the surgery had arrived—along with the presurgery X ray. The X ray showed that her colon had entirely healed. No surgery was necessary, and none was done, except to remove the bag.

The story doesn't end here, however. A few weeks later, the woman's daughter called me and asked if I would come to the hospital to be with the family again. Her brother had had a terrible motorcycle accident and had been in surgery all night. She hoped we could do some praising together on her brother's behalf.

I went to see him, along with his mother and sisters. I was told that he had had open heart surgery, surgery for his broken back, and several other very serious operations, all in one night. He was in the intensive care unit, completely immobilized and entirely unable to function. I'm not sure whether he was unconscious, but he was certainly not able to move, eat, or do anything for himself. The prognosis was, at best, an indefinite stay in the intensive care unit. One of the criteria for leaving the unit was being able to eat solid food, and that was clearly out of the question, indefinitely. At eighteen, it seemed his life was over.

Being very much "in practice" this time, the family and I gathered around him and praised God. Despite the recent miracle experienced by his mother, I could feel no hope for this young man. He was completely destroyed. This was one of those times when I was truly sure that if any healing was going to occur, it would have nothing to do with me or with my faith. I was going to pray and praise God out of obedience. I had to admit to the Lord that that was all I had.

I state this so flatly because many people tell me that a minister knows how to pray but they themselves cannot do it or do not have enough faith. However, like you and like Jehoshaphat, I have knowledge about the Lord and I have memories of the things I have seen the Lord do, but I still enter into the human condition of hopelessness. Much of the hopelessness comes from the realization that, humanly, I cannot do anything at all. When I realize just how dependent I am upon the Lord, it is always rather stunning. I have to command myself to remember the Lord's promises. Nevertheless, I pray.

Even a trained prayer must make use of obedience to face some of these difficult situations. Just standing in the intensive care unit surrounded by such misery is overwhelming, and you sometimes cannot see the glory of God right when you need it the most. It is, of course, always true that a human being could not be the agent of miraculous healing. I feel strongly that acknowledging that is an important part of healing prayer. That sense I had of being hopeless without God's action was both my human condition and one of the key elements of acknowledging just who has the power. By such means we can turn our helplessness into the beginning of praise.

Two days later, the family called again and wanted me to return to the hospital with them. I went. I was taken to a private room, and there was the young man, sitting up, feeding himself solid food, talking, laughing, and looking absolutely normal.

Thinking back on this experience, I understand something I had not before. I had spent a total of six hours in a car with the mother on the way to and from the hospital, plus two lengthy periods in the hospital with her and her son. I had walked beside her as she pushed his wheelchair. No one who had so recently been through her surgeries should have been so well and so completely unconcerned about her own health. You might expect her to dwell more upon her son than upon herself, but the thing was she did not even look sick. She did not move slowly. She was not pushing herself or otherwise hiding her own fatigue, pain, or discomfort. She was truly well. She had been healed, and I had seen that it was so with my own eyes.

Look at the place of praise in these healings. The songs the music group brought to our service certainly praised God. That praise helped many people's healings in the church that day. The sense of praise that the group took away with them made them talk about the service with their friends. That in turn resulted in my praying for the woman with the partial colostomy. The praises offered by the woman and her children resulted in her healing. The praises and the healing together resulted in my being called to pray for her son. The praise at the hospital resulted in a very substantial healing for him.

I hope and, in fact, believe that the praises helped him to a total healing. If a person never contacts me again, as with the son, often it turns out that that was a complete or even dramatic healing. Usually it is only when people don't get well that they go back to the doctor—or the person who prayed for them. In this case, I know that this family had a resource for healing that was effective for them—their praise—and I know that I was unnecessary to their use of it. That is why I think they kept praising and that the young man kept getting better.

This story illustrates the cascading nature of the effects of praising God and of the good effects of one healing upon another. We did of course ask the Lord directly to heal each of these people but then left off asking for something in order to dwell in God's praises. God did the rest. The Bible principle is this: God dwells in any place where his name is praised with sincere hearts. Let one of those places be your own situation of need or the need of someone you know, and do not hold back on praising God by yourself or with others who need healing.

Prayer Starter

"Praise you, Lord."

In Isaiah 6:3, the seraphim (heavenly beings) pray this prayer:

> *Holy, holy, holy is the Lord Almighty; the whole earth is full of his glory.*

Many people are familiar with this prayer, commonly known as the Sanctus (in Latin) or the Kaddish (in Hebrew). Since praise is central in Hebrew prayer, the Hebrew version is included below. This prayer has a particularly numinous and lovely quality in Hebrew. If you like to meditate, you might wish to learn it—even just the first half of it—as a centering prayer, repeating and repeating it to yourself. Repeating it for a few minutes (without thinking too hard about it but knowing its basic meaning) will focus you on the Lord. It will also focus your attention and emotion above the horizon of any earthly troubles. (Kevodo is really two words: *kevod* means "glory"; *o* means "his." In saying these words, the o's are long as in "Oh, my!" Otherwise, it reads as it looks.)

> *Kadosh, kadosh, kadosh,   Adonai Sabaoth. Milo kol ha-aretz kevodo.*

Chapter 9

Gabriel, Child from Heaven

The following story illustrates the function of being very specific when asking for healing. Being specific is not about telling God what to do but inviting him into the particular want and need in your life. Look at the way in which this worked for a couple I know.

At one time I had a church near a women's hospital, and sometimes the hospital people would call me to come and help someone. One day their social worker called and asked if I would contact a woman who was having surgery. It was a particularly desperate situation because they were about to end a pregnancy that had gone wrong to the point of extreme danger. The social worker gave me the woman's name and a number I could call. I promised to follow up. But first I had to wait a few hours until the anesthesia wore off before I could pray with her.

That evening I came home exhausted. I wondered how I was going to pull a prayer out the deficit of energy I was experiencing. I also wrestled with whether to call a person who did not know me and might still be too drugged to care. Despite all of this, I made the call. I reached the woman. I was sure she could not understand a word I said, but I prayed for healing and consolation for her and then hung up. Not knowing a thing about her except her name, I feared the prayer had been too impersonal or superficial. But I had done what I had promised.

Three months later, when I answered the office phone one afternoon, I heard a voice I did not know. The woman said for two months she had been calling every church of our name in the city phone directory, and there were quite a few. She was still searching for the right one. She was searching for whoever it was who prayed for her over the phone after her surgery at the women's hospital. The prayer had meant a great deal to her.

Having identified me, she and her husband came to my office to talk. They wanted to know how to come to a sense of resolution about having lost the child. There was some talk of a funeral, but there was no body, and it was awkward or impossible to invite people to such a service.

After several such visits, I began to understand that this was no ordinary event. Her ovaries had never functioned. The major grief was that against all medical tests and medical knowledge, she had conceived—only to lose the baby. But over a period of weeks, as she talked, what emerged was this: she had had no hope of ever conceiving a child, yet she had done so. The conception had been a miracle. She and her husband were deeply thankful for it. In fact, at last, they arrived quite firmly at that as their final "take" on the event. That gave a whole new atmosphere to our discussion about the service they wanted. It was to be something to mark this person's life, however brief. Above all, it was to thank God for this child and this conception. They'd named the baby Gabriel.

I was leafing through *The Book of Common Prayer* to find an appropriate service. There wasn't one. The page for "The Thanksgiving for the Adoption of a Child" fell open. I read through it. Slowly, it came to me that if I substituted the word conception for adoption, the entire thing was uncannily appropriate to them. After all, the primary thing was to recognize and thank God for the miracle of Gabriel's existence at all.

At this point it was just past Christmas. I'd had a life-sized baby-doll Jesus in the crèche near the altar, and it was still there. The couple and I chose an appropriate day on which to gather privately in the church. We thanked God for the conception of a child. At the end, I added a prayer for their baby, now in the arms of Jesus.

When the service was over, at the moment when other priests are able to say what I call a "pastoral platitude," I couldn't think of one. So many ministers and other people will say "have faith" or "have patience." Instead, I found myself praying one more prayer, quite unexpectedly—for "the new child to come." I took the doll out of the crèche, put it in the mother's arms, and said, "You remember this. You will have this some day." The odd thing is, neither of the parents thought this was odd. At least, it was positive imaging, and personal experience has taught me that positive imaging does do a great deal of good. In this case, I had felt this prayer and its accompanying action well up within me like a geyser, a great fountain not made of my own knowledge or emotion. I knew in my spirit that it was from the Lord. Nonetheless, I still always pray quickly before acting upon such an inspiration.

By now, you know that I believe in being this specific in our prayers for healing. That is my style and I find it sometimes works wonders. So my prayer with the doll from the crèche was spontaneous, but it was not just a thoughtless happenstance. In this particular case, it was a "word of power," a word given by the Lord. I say this carefully—because it can only be stated once you know the end result, in particular, whether it was constructive. Having said that, however, I believe this prayer was an instance of the gift of prophecy—one of the gifts of the Holy Spirit. (That is what a "word of power" is.) It is the Lord who speaks. He uses us to be the mouth sometimes, just as he uses our hands to feed other people.

There are groups of Christians to whom prophecy is a very familiar gift and others who think it is highly improbable in our age. I only report my own experience and leave it to you to decide what you think. The main thing, though, is that I emphasize the difference between my very limited human capacity and the divine capacity that may come through any of us at any time. In any case, the human being who is used in this way is not special; it is only God who is special, and we must never forget that.

Now back to praying very specifically for what we want: when we are specific, we are not telling God about something he does not already know. We are not trying to change God's mind. We are giving God dominion over that particular area of our life—including the fact that that is what we want. God wants our active invitation to come into this place in our life. He will accept the invitation. Once he does, God will do what God will do, and he will do it in his own time. Therefore it is not a contradiction to pray specifically and then also to wait expectantly for the outcome—an outcome that may be different, greater, earlier, or later than our request.

To return to Gabriel's parents, time passed, and the doctors continued to tell them that she would never have a child in the natural way. However, about three years later, she did become pregnant and carry to term twins—a double portion. This outcome seemed to echo Isaiah 61:1-3, 7, which says, "The Spirit of the Sovereign Lord . . . has sent me [the prophet] to bind up the brokenhearted, . . . to comfort all who mourn, and provide for those who grieve in Zion—to bestow on them a crown of beauty instead of ashes, the oil of gladness instead of mourning, and a garment of praise instead of a spirit of despair. . . . Instead of their shame, my people will receive a double portion . . . and everlasting joy will be theirs."

For most of the last decade, I have had the most extraordinary prayer relationship with the parents. Most of it has been long distance but full of the sense of the presence of God—and of the experience of praying for long years, only to feel that the answer had come quite suddenly.

This story illustrates the way in which God can enter into our life no matter what the situation. It also illustrates the major point of the Gospel. The Lord comes again, however inconceivable—like the in-conceivable children of the people whose story I just told you. As I have said elsewhere, healings are a sign that tells us we can believe in the ultimate healing of the world. With that sign comes our assurance that there is something beyond this world and beyond our grief and brokenness and loss. With this writing, I hand one such sign on to you.

This leads to one more blessing that Gabriel illustrates. When God heals, our time of grief and pain is turned into the occasion of the revelation of God's loving care and presence in our situation. In these parents' situation, real darkness was turned into the occasion of glory, thanksgiving, and fulfillment, and it happened three times over: The inability to conceive was turned into Gabriel. What would have been Gabriel's funeral became, after counseling, a time of thanksgiving and of the prophecy of a new child to come. And finally, their many years and dollars of doctors and no hope turned into a double portion of blessing.

Against the backdrop of impossibility the twins are more clearly the gift of God. If you need healing and have not received it—like Israel in captivity, you have not been forgotten. No matter how long the coming of the kingdom takes, surely the Lord is with you. Though you never see God in this world, one miracle child is yours, already and always in Jesus. I say this particularly to the many people who have called to ask me to pray for them to conceive a child, telling me how hopeless it has been. To them and to you I say, we can all, paradoxically, celebrate our darkness now before the second coming, while we are still captive to our hurts and to the disruptions of this world. The child from heaven has not forgotten us.

Prayer Starter

When you pray, be specific. Keep on praying, no matter how long the answer is in coming.

Find some reason to thank God in the very midst of the problem; look at the problem as the occasion for God's revelation of his care for you. For example:

> *Lord, send us a child. Thank you for the promise of healing. Thank you for this situation, since it is the occasion of your caring for us. Thank you for whatever the outcome is. Amen.*

Chapter 10

Paul's Hanky

A few years ago, my friend Margaret told me that a favorite friend of hers, Candice, was in the hospital with cancer. Not only was she very sick, but she was bitter. Margaret begged me to recommend something she could do for her friend. Knowing that a very sick person does not always appreciate company and sensing Candice could not be comforted with words, I kept wondering what potent or meaningful thing I could send her.

Mulling over Candice in prayer for a day, I remembered a passage in the New Testament book of Acts, where it says a very odd thing. During Paul's mission to the city of Ephesus, "God did extraordinary miracles through Paul, so that even handkerchiefs and aprons that had touched him were taken to the sick, and their illnesses were cured and the evil spirits left them" (Acts 19:11-12). I wished I could grab one of those handkerchiefs that had touched Paul and send it to Candice. If Paul did not think it was ridiculous for those people to steal his handkerchiefs (or sneak up on him with their own and touch him), why should I think so? Of course, I didn't have Paul to sneak up on. Never mind. It wasn't Paul who did those healings anyway; it was the Lord.

I did not think it was a coincidence that I had happened to think of this passage while praying for Candice. Perhaps the Lord was telling me what to do for her. I believe prayer is a very pragmatic thing. You ask God for what you need. You do whatever works; God will understand and do the right thing with it. Based on this conviction about prayer, I went out and bought a pretty, lacy handkerchief. I held it and prayed for Candice's healing—asking the Lord to treat the situation as if I were laying hands on Candice herself.

I then mailed the hanky to Margaret, with instructions. She was to read the passage in Acts, soak the handkerchief with her own prayer, and give it to her friend. If Candice was able to understand the nature and meaning of the handkerchief, Margaret should explain. That would make it a gift of prayers. If she was unable to understand, the Lord could use our prayers and good intentions and the handkerchief would at least seem to Candice to be a pretty gift; she could hold it and think of her friend.

A few days later Margaret called. She loved the idea and had prayed over the hanky. Margaret had then taken it to a large prayer group that was also praying for Candice. They too loved the idea and prayed over the handkerchief. They also took my instructions literally, soaking it with someone's holy water, carefully drying and folding it, and then taking it to Candice. They explained to her what they had done and what it meant.

Candice took a hold of that handkerchief and held on to it for dear life. From that moment until she left the hospital, she was seen clutching it, even when she was sleeping. No one could pry it out of her hand. It meant so much to her to have a tangible sign of everyone's prayers. It was as if the prayers themselves became concrete for her. She could not handle the extended effort at conversation that might have helped her unload her fears and receive comfort. However, she could lie in bed quietly and visualize the friends who had been involved, see them praying, see them soaking the cloth with holy water. All of the caring, the company of friends, and the religious community to which she would normally reach for comfort was embodied in that little piece of lace and cotton.

On her medications and with her degree of pain, Candice was unable to maintain the high degree of both rationality and concentration necessary to mentally absorb the medical steps required for her healing. Yet here was a single, simple, solid object easily grasped by even the foggiest mind and shakiest hand. It stood for the spiritual means of healing, a step toward healing that even a nonmedical person could carry out.

The effects I have just mentioned might be only emotional, only human, except for this: people's prayers do have effect and God does intervene. God would have heard and acted on the prayers of the community of faith, working in unity, regardless of whether Candice had had the emotional benefits of the handkerchief. However, in this case, the Lord used human nature—our built-in need for the concrete—to provide something that would provide immediate emotional comfort in a dire situation. Candice's friends knew right away that something had changed, because she suddenly stopped being bitter. And she got well.

I was astonished that the handkerchief had had any effect at all. No matter how many times it happens, I am always amazed when the Lord acts to heal someone. Yet I tell people always to remain expectant and await what the Lord will do. This is a strange dichotomy, to be sure. But an important part of expectancy is the knowledge of just whose presence you are expecting. There is a wonder, an astonishment, a holy awe, at every instance of God's presence and answer of prayer. While I expect, I have learned never to take for granted the answers the Lord will provide. Hence I am expectant but astonished when God acts.

In this case, I was further surprised by the overall effect of that handkerchief. I could not have designed the effect because so much of what happened was unpredictable: the way in which the prayer group had embraced the idea, Candice's reaction. So many elements were completely outside my control—the constructive effects, the unity among a group of Christians, and the general "more than the sum of the parts" character of the healing—that I realized that this healing had to be the Lord's own doing.

This was not magic. The mere concrete thing does not heal. The Lord does. The prayers comforted Candice and contributed to her healing. The prayerful, spiritual way the handkerchief was used made it a good symbol and, for that reason, a carrier of prayers. A physical object used in this spiritual way is what we call "sacramental." A sacrament is a physical object or action that is a sign that the Holy Spirit is working within you, such as the water used in baptism, or the bread and wine of communion.

The use of something material to represent God's action is deeply rooted in the religious cultures of the Bible. Hebrew thought tends toward the concrete. To the Hebrews and many other ancient peoples, everything they saw around them was a reminder of God's personal influence and intervention in their lives. The origin of saying a blessing before a meal is to acknowledge that very thing. Studying the passage in Acts, I realized that it must have seemed a wonderful idea to Paul for people to carry something tangible to their sick loved ones. They not only had with them the promise of God's spirit, but they also used something of God's creation to symbolize God's presence.

In the passage in Acts, "handkerchief" is actually a genteel mistranslation for what is, in the original Greek, "sweat rags." Paul supported himself by working with leather, which was hard work. The sweat rags were the head and neck bands he wore to absorb sweat, just as joggers do today. The rags and the aprons were his work clothes. Since Paul did this work to support his missionary effort and since it brought him into the community in a meaningful way, his work clothes were also his work-of-the-Holy Spirit clothes.

The passage in Acts is not unique in its focus on the concrete. In John's Gospel, Jesus heals a man who had been blind from birth. Jesus "spit on the ground, made some mud with the saliva, and put it on the man's eyes" (9:6). Then he told the man to wash in the pool of Siloam. When the man did so, "he came home seeing" (9:7). The use of mud by Jesus is most likely a reference to the Genesis 2 account of God creating human beings out of mud. Jesus identified his own work with that of the Creator. The man who had been blind from birth probably understood this reference, for the text says he had attended the synagogue and thus he likely had heard the Bible read there nearly every day. It is we who need to make this explicit for ourselves: if God created us, he can recreate us and fix anything that has gone wrong in the meantime.

Another biblical use of a physical thing to symbolize God's action is the practice of anointing with oil. Oil is a symbol both of healing and of the work of the Holy Spirit. In the Bible, oil was used to anoint kings. It was a sign that God had chosen them and that the Holy Spirit would work through them. Christians have long anointed with oil in connection with prayer for healing. Many denominations still do so today.

Before I had studied the Bible passages related to use of physical objects, I had the pastoral knowledge that something tangible might be comforting to the sick. Since then, the idea has burgeoned into a theological understanding. The idea that people were healed by touching Paul's garments is neither superficial nor superstitious. It is a profound theological statement about the right-now presence of the Lord among us. That presence would be among us with or without the physical thing. However, since faith is expressed in part by the way we use our possessions, it is not the least bit foreign to Christianity to use objects in this way. It must be understood, of course, that the healing comes from the Lord, not the object.

After thinking through all of the scriptural instances and the various pastoral and personal experiences I have had with the use of concrete things in healing, I have come to the conclusion that there are at least three reasons why the Lord uses physical things in the course of healing. First, as already noted, some things are designated as sacraments because of their use in Scripture and their use in the ancient church. When we use them, we are saying, in actions, that we wish to share with others the real presence of the Lord signified by those things.

Second, the Lord uses things and actions specifically for the psychological impact they may have on us. In Candice's case, it was the appropriateness of the handkerchief, representing prayer and healing, that was so important for emotional comfort. In other cases, a particular thing simply may be so meaningful to a person that it will aid in the healing process. The T-shirt in the story later in this chapter is an example of the psychological effect of an object building upon the already occurring spiritual healing. In yet other cases, when verbal communication has broken down between people, a gift or symbolic gesture may be instrumental in restoring communication.

Third, sometimes the object itself is an instrument of healing. For example, I had the experience of not being able to obtain a new prescription for reading glasses for an extended time. I only "happened" to get the eye exam, the new and better prescription, and the new glasses after it occurred to me to just sit down and pray for those things. It also happened that the particular experience of getting the eye exam and glasses had other healing effects upon me, so that getting the physical glasses—rather than, say, eyes that did not need glasses—was inherently important for me.

Of course, these three ways of using things for healing are not independent. They usually work together. And most important, the Lord's direct intervention is manifest with or without the aid of these things. For example, one day I decided to have the diamond from an old engagement ring put into a new setting. That marriage had ended seventeen years before, and the hurts associated with the marriage and divorce were long healed, as far as I could tell. I was only thinking the gem should probably not sit in a box for the rest of my life. I also had had an opportunity for a free appraisal. That was all—in the beginning.

I had the diamond set and put it on. Then something much greater occurred. All of a sudden a place very deep within me, related to the engagement, marriage, and divorce—some place I didn't even know I had—was healed. I felt a powerful peace, even an upwelling of love, in that place. It was not love of the man I had been married to, not in the sense of marriage love. It was God's love within me, somehow reaching out in the direction of that man. It was a complete surprise brought about by a mere thing, one that I had once considered to have sacramental meaning. I had thought that that diamond's sacramental meaning had been denied or canceled. Yet a sacramental sort of meaning suddenly returned, different now but very clear. I had been left with a gift from that marriage, something of real purity and intrinsic value, something more than material.

I have used this type of tool for healing only a few times, but occasionally it has been a life saver. In one of my parishes, a teenage girl was hospitalized in the mental ward because she had tried to kill herself. The situation was heartbreak enough for the family, but then something else happened that made it worse. After lengthy counseling, the daughter told the counselor that her father had molested her in her early years. The counselor was legally required to report this to the police but had not yet done so. The family called, desperate for help. If charges were filed, the father's reputation would be ruined. In a small town, the family's income and business would be a thing of the past, and generations of involvement in that community would come to a humiliating and bitter end. Even if the charges were dropped, they could never recover from the stigma.

I went to visit the family. Both parents, their older children, and I sat around the table and talked. From a knowledge of the family and that conversation, I was certain the father could not have molested his daughter. Apart from all else, the family told me that in those years the father had always been either at work or at home with the mother and siblings together. There was no time when he could have abused his daughter. I was certain this was correct. Nevertheless, I prayed that God would have mercy on us all and do whatever was right in this situation.

The family desperately wanted me to do something. So I asked them to take me to the daughter's room. There we all sat in a circle and prayed for her. After a few minutes, I asked whether there was anything, maybe a piece of clothing, that was special to her, something they would be allowed to bring to her in the hospital. Unanimously they identified her favorite T-shirt. They took it out of a dresser drawer and handed it to me. I laid it in the center of our prayer ring and asked them to lay hands on it. I told them I wanted them to take her a token of the family's caring—

something that would mean caring to her—but first I wanted them to soak it with their prayers for her and for the resolution of this situation. I wanted them to clothe her with the power of prayer. Maybe the Lord would act somehow through those prayers. What exactly the Lord would do, I didn't know, but God would do something.

While they prayed over the T-shirt, I added something in silence. I quietly prayed the exorcism prayer. There was real evil here, out of control. By this I do not mean the girl was evil; rather, the situation was evil, and the daughter was as much a victim of it as her family was. Silently, I cast out whatever the evil was, in the name of Jesus, throwing all my heart into the prayerful determination that no spiritual tool should be withheld from this teenager or her family. After all, the book of Ephesians says to put on the whole armor of God to defend against the "powers of this dark world and against the spiritual forces of evil in the heavenly realm" (Ephesians 6:12). I was not sure there were "forces of evil" in the sense of independent spiritual personages. But if God had inspired this biblical text, God would understand my meaning in using it. I intended to provide all of the armor of God for this young woman.

A couple of hours later, the family took the T-shirt to the daughter. In this case I had told them to say nothing about praying over the shirt, since that might seem to her like mere manipulation. It had been a power-filled and truly holy time of intercession, but I did not think she would understand the spiritual significance of praying over the shirt. However, I knew that the family's genuine love would be made concrete for her, without words, by their bringing her favorite shirt to her. I had also encouraged them not to talk about the accusation of abuse. That would only be inflammatory and would distract from the message of love. A symbol of love with no words and no implied demand for gratitude or anything else is often the most effective way of communicating humanly. In this case, it would also communicate God's love, because we had prayed for God's own intervention.

The family followed my instructions. It turned out that this was exactly the simply-loving thing that had effect. About four hours later, I received a call from the family. They had taken the shirt. She had put it on immediately. Two hours after that—all on her own—she had told the hospital staff that the accusation of molestation had not been the truth. She explained that she had not really meant to lie. The counselor had kept pressing for any evidence of molestation, over and over again. She had not been able to get away from the subject. Finally, longing for love and attention even from the counselor, she had wrongfully agreed there was abuse. For a while the comfort and conciliation on account of "what had happened to her," the supposed abuse, had seemed to her like love. But it was not. Real love was her family. They had cared about her anyway, even bringing her favorite shirt. She wanted the story about her father stopped.

The counselor resigned from the case, admitting to having pressed too hard. The accusation had not been reported to the police. The crisis was over.

Shortly thereafter the daughter returned home. She went to college and got on with her life. The family as a whole had received a substantial healing. The combination of the timing— which was most certainly beyond the control of any one person involved in the situation—and the lasting nature of the healing marks this as more than a human resolution.

The T-shirt is certainly not for every situation. Paul's hand-kerchief is not for the average situation. So here are some suggestions for beginners and for everyone else who would like to try the "hanky" type of prayer. First, prayer is pragmatic; do what works for you. It's important, however, that you not impose your spirituality on others. If holy water or the T-shirt idea is special to you, use it to pray by yourself for another person, but do not force it on others when you are praying with them. If you force it, you will only convey the message that you are playing God, not the message of caring. Ask what is meaningful for the others, or ask whether your prayer idea is OK with them. In the situations described in this chapter, I merely presented the basic idea.

That the other people embraced and used it—and in the first case went much further with it—shows that that prayer really did grow out of their situation.

If a needed healing in your life is being hindered by a lack of communication for any reason, you might want to look for something that will mean God's presence to you. Ask the Lord to show you what will be both meaningful and effective for you (or the person for whom you are praying). Or look to your own religious tradition or the Bible for the use of objects in prayer. Always be sure to acknowledge the Lord's presence and work in this process.

Prayer Starter

Sit at the dinner table and before you eat, while you are still hungry, look around at everything you see. Read the creation story in Genesis 1. On what day of creation would each of the things on the table have originated? Think how concretely they represent God's intervention in your life right now. Eat with reverence, knowing that all of it is a gift of God, as an intervention for healing—that is, to keep you healthy—in your life right at this very moment. Thank God for the food, the table, the various other things around you, and God's intervention in your life.

Chapter 11

Two Resurrections

In the course of ministry, I have come to know a number of funeral directors. Many of them have an unusual empathy with people, and just as many are very faithful in their relationships with God. Curious, I asked one of them about this. His story and the others in this chapter demonstrate one thing: no one is too hopeless or too rejected by God or humankind to be healed. Everyone is invited to reach for healing, to reach for the personal touch of Jesus Christ, and even if we cannot reach far enough, it is his will to reach out to us.

Here is the story the funeral director told:

> Many years ago I was in the hospital, paralyzed and very sick. To top it off, I had the most awful itch on my back. It was driving me crazy. One day that itch got so bad I absolutely could not stand it. I willed with all my mental might to scratch that itch, but I could do nothing. Finally, I tried to comfort myself by thinking about Bible stories. I had always liked that one about the woman who touched the hem of Jesus' robe and her flow of blood was healed, so I started to imagine it, and the imagination became very, very real to me. I could identify with that woman, how much she wanted just to touch Jesus—if only his garment. I wanted so much for her to be able to reach far enough through that crowd. Then, in my imagination—as in the story—she stretched her hand as far as ever she could and did just reach the edge of his robe. And she was healed.

Suddenly I came to myself and realized something: at the moment when I had been so much in that story, when the woman had finally touched him, I too had reached out—physically. I found myself scratching that itch on my back until I was satisfied and it was gone. Then I realized that I, too, was healed.

From that day, my paralysis has been gone.

For the funeral director, this experience was the reason he believed in God and the reason he had decided to go into one of the caring professions. His story—in biblical terms—falls under the category of resurrection. In the Gospels, there is a group of healing stories in which the people healed are not literally dead, but their productive life is over. Their family life and social life are also over. The funeral director's productive life was over until his healing. And so with the woman who touched Jesus' robe.

The healing of the woman with the flow of blood is introduced in the middle of another healing story in Luke 8. That other healing is a resurrection. Look what happens: a ruler of the synagogue named Jairus falls at Jesus' feet and pleads with him to come to the ruler's home to heal his dying daughter (8:41-42). Before Jesus has a chance to go with Jairus, a messenger comes with the news that the daughter has already died. Jesus goes to Jairus' house anyway. The people there are mourning, wailing out loud as was their custom.

The mourners are described as "knowing that she was dead," but Jesus nonetheless tells them to "stop wailing. She is not dead but asleep" (8:52, 53). To modern, Western readers, Jesus' words seem to suggest that this might not be a resurrection story. However, in the Bible, sleep is often used to refer to death. When Jesus goes to the girl, takes her hand, and says, "My child, get up!" he calls her back into the life of this world. The end of the story makes clear that this is a resurrection: "Her spirit returned [note, returned], and at once she stood up" (8:55).

The story of the woman with the flow of blood occurs between the announcement of the girl's death and Jesus' trip to Jairus's house. Luke's purpose in embedding the woman's story in this way is to emphasize that it exemplifies resurrection—resurrection of a particularly urgent kind, resurrection from a living death.

The woman's layers of uncleanness—hopelessness added to hopelessness so that there can be no question about her official "rejection" by God—make her the victim of a living death. She is rejected on many levels. In the first century, a Jewish man did not approach, much less touch, a woman to whom he was not related. Women generally were thought to be low on God's list. There also is a complex of laws in the Bible, mainly in Leviticus, that says that a woman with any flow of blood, healthy or unhealthy, is officially unclean. Anything she touched became unclean. No one who was unclean could go into the temple or offer sacrifice until going through rites of purification. The unclean woman's perceived rejection by God was actually considered contagious. A sick person was often regarded as being punished by God for sin and thus was socially suspect. No one would live with the woman with the twelve-year flow of blood, and she should not even have been allowed on that crowded street.

The message of the woman's healing in this story is that a person's life can be resurrected. Not only does Jesus care about people, he also is able and willing to make out of their situations a sign of God's presence and love. The condition of living death includes those who are locked in depression, addiction, terminal illness, or other seemingly endless, hopeless conditions. Those very people, because of their infirmity, because their life is in some sense over, can become the occasion of others' encounters with God. In a way they become the locus of the presence of the Lord: "Your body is a temple of the Holy Spirit" (1 Corinthians 6:19). God can be found there by others—no matter how badly off the living dead are at this moment.

It is important to focus on this because too many of us are sure we are God's rejects—either for our own private reasons or because society has made sure we are treated that way. Such a person, like this woman, comes to have no function in the world. He or she is, in society's view, "beyond help," beyond grace. Some of the first people who contracted HIV were seen that way. They desperately wanted to have the solace and hope that going to church would bring them. Many of them could demonstrate that their illness was not because of something they had done, and these included children. Nevertheless, people regarded them as sinful, and sermons were preached to that effect. Churches kicked them out. The message was: You are not just sick; you are a carrier of real evil. We don't want to look at you, and we certainly do not want to be with you. The "official" side of religion, part of organized Christianity, declared them outcast. They were not permitted in the temple.

Of course, no matter how they contracted the virus, they, like all of us, were sinful and God wanted to heal and console these people. But the other people were so afraid of being contaminated that they not only refused to help but condemned those who were in need. Ironically, in a way, the "well" people did become contaminated—with evil—by means of their own ungodly actions. When Jesus condemned those who had seen him sick or in prison and had not helped him (Matthew 25:41-46), his disciples objected that they had never seen him in such conditions. "I tell you the truth," he responded, "whatever you did not do for one of the least of these, you did not do for me" (Matthew 25:45). Not showing mercy to some such person is ungodly, but worse, it is a rejection of Jesus himself.

I experienced the depth of people's rejection of the sick when I was asked to pray for one of the first AIDS patients in the United States. I was told very quietly that no one else would visit this man, near death in a hospital. No one knew much about AIDS then, but I knew enough to be afraid, mortally afraid, of what he had. But I could not bear the thought that he might die alone, without prayer, without human love or a sign of God's love.

I went. I looked at him, lying alone, unconscious. Normally I lay on hands when I pray for a sick person. Besides the biblical basis for this, studies show that human touch is healing and comforting. I prayed hard and fast about what to do. A distinct intuition came to me: don't be afraid of this man. Then it occurred to me that not to pray for him and not to place my hand on his shoulder while I did so was more like evil than this poor man's disease might seem, because it would be my unholy choice not to pray. So I prayed, with my hand on his shoulder. I prayed for God to be with him and to let him know that people still loved him.

Years later, we learned that AIDS cannot be transmitted by touch. I was so glad I had prayed for the man before he died. When you consider Matthew 25, it was, after all, Jesus for whose sake I had been offering healing prayer in the first place. Luke intentionally chooses the lowest-of-the-low to demonstrate the power of Jesus the healer as well as the availability of God's grace to the very least of us. The very least can become the sign and occasion of God's presence in the world and a demonstration project for the kingdom of heaven. The reason I prayed for the AIDS patient is that no one is God's reject. I must not presume, through ignorance or fear, to go God one better and ignore others. If God could love the woman with the flow of blood, I could pastorally love that dying man in the hospital. Ironically, his supposed rejection-by-God (as society thought then) would be contagious if I withheld from him the human signs of grace. I would become the unclean one.

That is the sort of decision Jesus makes when he seeks out and speaks to this woman in Luke 8. Because of the social customs and the religious law of the day, officially the woman commits a social outrage and a great sin by touching Jesus' robe. Notice what Jesus does: after she is healed, but before she comes forward, he seeks her out. He is determined to find her. He speaks to her, breaking the social and religious codes too. He effectively approves her touching his garment—though officially he is now unclean, unacceptable in the temple. In Jesus' view, she has done only right, and God is with her. God chose to heal her, so in his sight, she is clean.

Everyone who saw her after this would know. The healing took place not in a corner but out in public, among a large crowd, all of whom were straining to hear and see what Jesus would do. Forever marked—that is what she is at the end of the story. But for a different reason than before. She is now well, acceptable in society, and ritually, religiously clean. Jesus gave her that. The "contagion" reversed itself; instead of her uncleanness attaching itself to Jesus, his holiness attaches itself to her. Wherever she goes, her presence will preach what Jesus did.

I suspect that she represents even more than that. There is only one other person in the Gospels who bleeds—Jesus himself bleeds on the cross. Reference to his blood is made in the accounts of the Last Supper, where Jesus says that there will be a "new covenant" because of his blood. In Luke 8, the meaning of the woman's bleeding has been reversed. It is now the sign and occasion of the power of God—the purifying power of God—in her body. It is that purification that Jesus is offering to his disciples when he refers to the "new covenant in my blood." His offer of purity does not depend on us but only on his sacrifice.

Stories like that of the woman with the flow of blood are intended to tell us that there is absolutely no one who is ineligible for resurrection, be it resurrection from a living death in this life or resurrection in the kingdom of heaven. It is God's decision to reach out to touch us with his healing power. Though the woman reached for Jesus' robe, there is a real sense in which God did the reaching. The next resurrection account illustrates this.

My friend Kay had a leg amputated because of a dire illness. Physically, in so far as it was possible, she recovered. But she was certain the rest of her life was going to be a living death. She was paralyzed by depression, and she was terrified—terrified to get up and use her crutches. Terrified she would fall. She could only lie in bed, look out at the sky, and hope to die. Surely God had rejected her. There was no hope.

One night she fell asleep in just such a state of depression. She dreamed a hand reached down to her. She felt she was being called and pulled upward to grasp that hand. If she could only just reach and touch it . . .

In the dream, she did reach, and she did touch that hand. Then she woke up. Something was different. No longer depressed, no longer afraid, she sat up, tried out her crutches, and discovered she could walk. From that night on, she was as able to go where she wished as anyone I know.

Kay received resurrection from living death. My funeral director colleague received a resurrection from living death. The woman with the flow of blood did, as well. All of these healings are a sign for us of the reality of the resurrection in the life to come. And that resurrection, like theirs, is the pure gift of God. There is no one who is too low down for God to reach or too small for God to seek out.

Prayer Starter

If you can't pray or if your best efforts yield nothing you can see, a physical analogy to prayer sometimes primes the pump. This technique is especially good for children because it is concrete. (Jesus did say we should be like little children in our relationship with him.) Use this method to try being a child in your worship:

Stand alone in a quiet room and reach. Reach as high as you can. Then reach to the floor. (If you cannot do these things, sit quietly and reach with your mind.) This much of the exercise is enough for some people, especially if it is repeated. To go further with it, pretend or visualize that you are actually reaching to touch Jesus.

While you do this, address the Father in heaven, praying:

Where are you? I want to seek you with all of my heart and reach into every part of me to find you. Thank you for wanting to be found, even by the least of us. Now please reach down and find me and heal me. Thank you that you have already said that you want to do this, even for the least of us. Amen.

Chapter 12

Manna Faith Manifest: Healing Sustenance

The moment when I most concretely came to know that God will provide for me represents a powerful healing of life. Not only were my physical needs healed, but I was healed of a sense of abandonment that was all-pervading.

Before this incident, I had never thought of Jesus' promise of sustenance as a promise of healing. In the Gospel of John, Jesus declares, "I am the bread of life. He who comes to me will never go hungry, and he who believes in me will never be thirsty. . . . Everyone who looks to the Son and believes in him shall have eternal life" (6:35, 40). In addition to providing for our physical nourishment, Jesus provides for our eternal sustenance, our life with God. The key to both is to look to the Lord for all that we need. Remember, he said, "I am the bread of life."

At the time I became aware of God's provision, I had been married for almost ten years and had recently moved to a beautiful historic house. My husband and I had barely finished restoring it when one day I came home from a short business trip to find that my husband had left me without any warning whatsoever. We had not been arguing about anything in particular, and our life had seemed to be one of long-term commitment—if only because we had recently moved and heavily invested ourselves in the restoration.

I was shattered, but it was not until I moved into another, much smaller house of my own four months later that the full significance of the situation hit me. In those four months, every person who had been a support for me was in some way gone. My counselor of many years happened to be away for the summer. Also, a vacuum was created because I left the parish I had loved so much. I had not wanted to leave. But every time I was near my old parish, people asked me about my divorce. While I knew they asked because they cared, it was a great pain for me to discuss it. I just could not deal with that. This change of parishes was not easy for me because ordination was my dearest-held hope (and had been for twenty years). I feared I might have to give up the ordination process.

My family simply could not face what had happened to me. In their presence I felt as if I had done something terribly wrong or had some fearful communicable disease. (Only some years later did I understand that their turning away occurred because my family could not bear to face my pain. Also, they felt responsible, having wanted so much for me to marry this particular man.) My old friends kept at a distance when I moved into a very run-down, definitely untrendy neighborhood. It was not easy getting people to come across town to visit me.

During this time I could not find a handle on something positive to which I might cling during my time of crisis. I was stuck— and scared beyond anything most people can imagine. I was succumbing to a deep depression and a kind of desperation of soul that no one can understand without having been through it.

The weekend I moved into my new home, my checkbook registered zero. Exactly. But it couldn't; it must be wrong. If only I could get some rest and some food, I would see that. But I had little food. Having downsized for moving, I had brought with me only two items of food: a single bag of rice and a few tea bags. On Sunday, I ate the rice. On Monday, I would refigure my checkbook to see if there was a mistake, and I would buy groceries.

Monday morning came. I figured and figured and re-added that checkbook. It was not a mistake. It said, firmly, zero. Exactly. Undeniably. Absolutely. Zero. And I owned only tea bags.

By this time it was almost 11 a.m. I was getting more desperate than ever. I found out that I couldn't get an advance on my paycheck no matter what, and payday was two full weeks away. All of my credit cards were unusable because they were held jointly with my husband and the divorce was still in process. I couldn't find my family on the phone or in person. (Much later, I learned that they were collectively camped out at the hospital, where my aunt was having surgery, something with which they had not wanted to burden me.) It didn't occur to me to go to the church I had begun attending and ask them for money. So here I was, a middle-class, thirty-one-year-old woman with a Ph.D., a wonderful job, a good salary, department-store clothes, a car of my own—and absolutely nothing to eat and no hope of getting anything for two whole weeks.

Having exhausted all of the rational approaches and with no resources, I knew of nothing that could possibly help me. Then an idea related to physical feeding came to me. Israel had been hungry in the desert, and God had sent them manna.

Of course, that sort of thing didn't happen today. But it was an idea. I looked around me, though I had an office to myself, just to be absolutely sure no one could possibly see me and laugh. Then I deliberately sat down in my office chair and only because I had read about it in the Bible, asked God if I could have some manna. I figured asking couldn't hurt, but I expected nothing.

At 11:00, I decided to go upstairs to the lounge to check the mail and get some of the unlimited, fresh-ground coffee. It was not food, but it was something. I went by the mail room. There was no mail for me. I walked into the lounge, toward the coffee pot. Someone I barely knew came in carrying a big, round deli-type tray. On it was exactly one huge roast beef sandwich. "Here. This is for you," he said, handing me the tray and then leaving without further conversation.

Reverently, I ate the sandwich. I did not yet think of it as manna, though—not then. It had always been the custom that when food was left over from a meeting, it was brought to the lounge for whoever wanted it. The implication was that a lunch meeting had ended and this was what was left. (It had not yet occurred to me that it was extremely peculiar for a lunch meeting to be over by 11:00.)

I had no idea where dinner would come from, but at least I had had one substantial and healthy thing that day. Dinnertime came. Someone I had not seen for years had come into town and asked if I would accept being taken to dinner. Yes, I would.

After that, each day at mail time, I deliberately prayed for manna, checked my mail, went to the lounge, and got some coffee. Each day something happened to provide food for my lunch. In many cases it turned out to be the leavings of meetings. It was always something different and always just enough. Each day at dinnertime, something unusual happened, always something different, and again, just enough. This continued for seven days.

The next week there were no more lunch-providing meetings, and every out-of-town friend had already (coincidentally) shown up. No more dinners. I was beginning to have that desperate, sinking sense in my stomach again.

Nevertheless, by this time I had reflected upon my prayer for manna. I decided that it was a prayer from within the wilderness—and from deep hunger that was more than physical. I did not yet have faith that manna-type miracles could occur today. The world outside of me would have to cooperate in such a miracle, and I just couldn't see that happening.

Yet difficult though it was, I made myself sit down in that chair one more time. I had to survive until Friday, and God was my only source of bread. I prayed for manna, this time apologizing to the Lord because I did not believe it was going to come. I went upstairs. No coffee. I went to the mail room. One letter, from my bank. I knew what it must say: my account was either overdrawn or closed because the balance had gone to zero. I came close to throwing the envelope away, but out of obligation I opened it. Inside was a letter that said someone had anonymously deposited $5000 in my account.

Who could it have been? After thinking hard I had an idea. Some days earlier, immediately after my move, I had attended a morning wedding. The reception wasn't to be until much later, and an older guest there with nowhere to go had wanted to sit down somewhere. I had offered my house. Though it was piled with boxes and I was very much humiliated by my change in physical circumstances, I thought it was right that I should offer. After all, I myself felt so much out in the cold. As I checked off everyone who might want to give me anything, she was the only person I could think of who was unaccounted for.

I called her. I was right. And she didn't mind being discovered, because she wanted to tell me why she had given me the gift. When she had seen my house, she had thought, "I have always lived with family. I have always dreamed of a place that was only mine—a little house on a cobblestone street. Just like yours! It was so much like the daydream I have carried around for forty years. The only difference between your house and my daydream house is that yours doesn't have a shower. I thought you should put one in. It would sort of complete the dream I had."

With this one statement, she contributed to my healing beyond anything she might have guessed. Suddenly my little house in the run-down neighborhood was a "magic house."

I bought groceries. I later arranged for the shower and had about $2,000 left over. With that $2,000 and my salary, I was able to live quite well for the rest of the winter.

I had experienced manna and then an abundance beyond belief in the midst of a thick darkness. That jolted me right out of the worst of my fears and into the beginning of emotional and spiritual recovery. With this experience, I had a new, solid ground upon which to stand: the Lord himself.

After that, circumstances were sometimes desperate, but *I* was never again desperate. I always prayed for manna, and it always came. Two years later I was ordained and, because of my manna experience, I had the courage to give up a good salary for the lower income of a priest. I knew God would provide. And God did provide, in a cascading series of money-from-out-of-the-yonder, gifts, food, and even plants appearing on my doorstep, left by unseen hands. Sometimes I knew the human source, and sometimes I never did.

Eventually, out of the original darkness and emptiness, another miracle occurred. I started, out of nowhere, to be asked to preach. The first time I stepped into a pulpit on a Sunday at 11:00 and looked out over three hundred and fifty people, something within went "snap!" Suddenly I knew that this was my calling within my calling, always intended for me. But I had only preached once before and had had no training in preaching. This simply appeared out of nothing, like creation. I now understand that my preaching arose from two sources. First, I had been so empty of all of my previous creative and social outlets that my inner self had literally stored up a powerhouse of energy and need. A sort of geyser burst forth, a geyser of the Word and of the Holy Spirit. This would never have happened if I had remained comfortable in my old circumstances.

Second, I realized that I would never have had the opportunity to preach while I had been married. People had thought of me as shy and small, not the sort of person you would invite into the pulpit at all. I had always encouraged my husband to be at the center of attention at church and everywhere else. So—on the Feast of the Transfiguration, August 6, 1982—I discovered in a whoosh that there had been a powerful point to my being sprung, however much against my will, from a relationship in which I was not going to fulfill my calling.

This was a great shock, because it seemed to contradict my ideal of marriage. The only way I can understand it is through Romans 8:28, "in all things God works for the good of those who love him." God can use even an unwilling divorce for the good of the believer. I also now know that if you embark upon a journey with the Lord, you are going to go through some substantial wildernesses. Most important, though, you are going to end up where the Lord wants you, regardless of where you thought you were going.

The sacrifice of Jesus, and his Spirit within us, provide manna for today. That sometimes includes manna for this very day. Jesus also provides what I call "manna faith," and that was the real healing in this experience. My inner self had been shattered by being left entirely alone with absolutely nothing. My sense of self was restored because regardless of whoever did not love me, God did. I had been issued a new charter, so to speak. I changed to a radical, no-holds-barred reliance on God to sustain me. And it was fun. I became truly free, free of fear, a prisoner released in an important way from the cares of this world.

Today I would not trade my experience in the wilderness with no food for any amount of money. I have become "independently wealthy" because I have the potential for manna, a widow's jar of oil that can never run out (see 2 Kings 4:1-7). Every time it occurs to me to wonder whether there is actually a resurrection, the life Jesus promised, I think there must be. God's resources are unlimited.

As for healing—I had believed, before this experience, that the Lord could work a change within me to heal me. What I had not been able to grasp was that the Lord can and does change circumstances and the actions of other people, the world, to do his life-sustaining work for us. The Lord had worked the world like a piece of clay so that without disrupting what other people needed or received, he also provided for me. There is no circumstance that is beyond God's healing power, no condition of life out of which the Lord cannot heal you. To put it another way, nothing and no one can get in the way of your healing. It may sometimes feel as if the world is out to get you and the world is most certainly bigger than you, but the Lord is bigger than all of it. You just have to go to him directly with your needs. That is the key to everything.

Prayer Starter

My prayers for manna were based on total desperation—a personal wilderness—and one other thing: a sense that the Bible was my invitation to go out and find the God who is described in there.

Find a model in the Bible (see below) and read the passage. Then read it again, placing your own name in the place of the person who was healed or sustained by God's gifts.

Here are some examples of passages you might want to use:

1 Kings 17:7-16. You are the widow of Zarephath and Elijah proclaims God's unfailing provision for you.

2 Kings 4:1-7. You are the widow and Elisha prophesies God's gifts to you.

Exodus 16. Relive the story of the provision of manna and quail with yourself as one of the starving Israelites.

Luke 5:1-10. You are Simon Peter, tired and desperate after a night of profitless fishing; Jesus announces your overflowing catch.

Chapter 13

Inner Healing:
Your Body Is the Temple
of the Holy Spirit

Some years ago, I saw a movie in which two men robbed a bank and held everybody there hostage. The situation got out of hand, and there was no good solution. Negotiations went on and on. The robbers and the hostages started to get hungry, which aggravated the situation. One robber, with a distinctly deranged look in his eyes, became increasingly anxious and kept saying, "Maybe we should just finish everybody off now."

His partner tried to calm him down before things got worse. He suggested they request some food and drinks from the police as part of the negotiations. "Maybe a beer will help your nerves," he said.

Outraged, the deranged robber shouted, "Absolutely not! I never put drugs in my body. Your body is the temple of the Holy Spirit."

The other robber looked even more scared when he heard that. And well he might. With that last sentence, his partner showed how completely out of touch with reality he was. This was a robbery, after all—hardly evidence of a religious orientation. He didn't want to put drugs in his body, but he was willing to kill people.

Though most of us are nothing like this robber, the story demonstrates two mistakes that ordinary people make all the time. The first has to do with what makes us godly or ungodly. In Matthew 15:8-11, Jesus quotes Isaiah 29:13: "These people honor me with their lips, but their hearts are far from me," and then goes on to say, "Listen and understand. What goes into a man's mouth does not make him 'unclean,' but what comes out of his mouth, that is what makes him 'unclean.'" "What comes out of the mouth" does not refer only to what we say; it also refers metaphorically to our total effect on other people, that is, to whatever we do.

So for the robber to avoid drugs is fine, but he is still "unclean," that is, ungodly, because of what else he is saying and doing. I have so often heard people say that once you are saved, it doesn't matter what you do; you are still acceptable to God. Of course, God continues to love every person. But the major point the New Testament makes about this is that once you are saved, you are empowered—and obligated—to try to live a godly life. Paul writes in Romans 8:12 that because we have been granted salvation, "we have an obligation—but it is not to the sinful nature, to live according to it . . . but if . . . you put to death the misdeeds of the body, you will live" with Christ. Both are true: we are saved and loved by God, but we also are supposed to participate in our salvation—to demonstrate our love of God—by the way we live. When Paul tells us our body is the temple of the Holy Spirit (1 Corinthians 6:19), he makes the same point.

The second common mistake has to do with the role of the Holy Spirit within us. The Holy Spirit is supposed to be our life guide. In this role, the Spirit creates and nurtures our moral choices and the godliness of our behavior. Being guided by the Spirit is not just a passive matter, however. We are provided with an "engine" for good (the Holy Spirit), and we are to strive to live up to the standard of godliness, to honor the Spirit within us.

Now we get to one of the most important connections between the Holy Spirit and healing. Spiritual illness, as opposed to physical or emotional illness, is characterized by ungodly behavior. Of course, all of us receive the Holy Spirit in our baptism; so we all have the capacity for spiritual health, but that does not mean we always allow that good capacity to run our lives. See, for example, Romans 7, where Paul describes his inability to do the good he wants to do. Like Paul, most of us begin by regarding this obligation as a matter of trying. Then we find out that it takes more than that, that it takes a spiritual healing.

To understand this, we have to understand that our spiritual illness can originate either with outright sinful choices or with the harmful effects of the sin of the world. Most of us do our best to be good. However, deep inside of us there are places that have been injured and need healing. No human medicine or treatment can get all the way inside there, and most of the time even if those hurts can be reached, they are much too tender to touch. Those injured inside places are the origin of much of what we do that is wrong on the outside, whether it is an unhealthy use of drugs, robbing a bank, or the inability to begin and stay in a healthy marriage.

Here is where the two bank robbers are relevant. The one who only wanted to get some money is making a choice to do wrong. The deranged one is making the same choice. However, we would usually refer to the way in which the latter did it as "sick." This is literally so; within him are controlling forces that are in the realm of illness. With most of us, the hurts are not in the extreme category of illness, but they still control our behavior from within. The result of such hurts is an inner bondage, an unconscious "set" that powerfully determines our actions. You cannot just tell a person, "Don't do that." The person may not have control over the inward hurts that often drive such behavior.

An obvious case is that of child abuse. An abused child heals on the outside, but the heart of the child shatters, unable to trust and love in the way we are meant to. It has been documented that even while an abused person is conscious of the source of past hurts, he or she may pass on that abuse to the next generation. The hurts must express themselves somehow. Sometimes those of us who do not turn the effects of the hurt outward will turn those effects inward, resulting in depression, physical illness, or both. Changing ungodly behavior often requires healing inner hurts.

Instead of dwelling on what we are not supposed to do on the outside, let us dwell on bringing the power of the Holy Spirit to bear on the inside. The Spirit is already within every Christian. Why not use the Holy Spirit as an inner engine of health to find, touch, and heal all of those places that are injured within? Inner healing is a remedy for broken hearts.

Each of us is the temple of the Holy Spirit. The Spirit within us has a very particular relationship with the hurts of the past. The Spirit witnesses within us that we are not alone and that Jesus is Lord of our temple. We are God's house. The very least and most sinful person can claim this wonderful distinction. By the power of the Spirit, we always carry Jesus the healer with us. One of the central principles of inner healing is that the Lord has access to our innermost selves and even to hurts that are unknown to us. Our task is to let him heal them.

For some people, a little reflection and prayer can do wonders. However, for others, it is more difficult, and it may be useful for a therapist to guide them through to healing. My first experience of inner healing, a spontaneous one, showed me what God-within-me can do. It was this healing not available by any other route that showed me, in later life, how to help other people.

When I was a teenager, my parents divorced. During the eighteen months after my mother's announcement of the divorce, things became covered with a darkness that I could not penetrate. I went through a bout of rather serious depression, gradually becoming incapacitated.

Because my family did not talk about the situation and because I had managed to continue to do well in school, the entire effect on me remained unarticulated and unrecognized. On the first day of ninth grade, however, I went into a desperate tailspin. It was as though I had been standing perilously on tiptoe without knowing it and a wind came and knocked me right over.

I had been placed in an advanced math class, which was something to look forward to. Yet the trigger of the new desperation came from that class, from the math teacher, whose first words to us were "I hate kids." The other kids knew exactly how to respond. From day one, they played practical jokes on her. In return, she took that out on us collectively, which seemed unfair to me. I didn't have the capacity for practical jokes, nor would I ever sass the teacher or disobey. And my marks were important to me. Grades were my bank account for college. I neither knew how, nor was inclined, to take out my hurt on the other people involved. So where the others aimed their hurt outward, mine went inward.

Each day the teacher would begin the class by asking one after another of us if we had done our own homework. When a student answered, "Yes," she would ask, "Are you sure? Can you prove it?" and on and on until the person broke down. Sometimes she would start by giving a test unrelated to what we were currently studying. Through all of this, something within me fought to stay on top of things.

Within a few weeks, however, my already raw insides took over, and I was sick every single morning before school. Math class was first period, and I would wake up riveted on the expectation of what that teacher would do next. By this time, the teacher had begun asking questions like, "What is two plus two?" When she asked me, not one word would come out of my mouth. I couldn't defend myself. I missed twenty-one days of school in a relatively short period. I was alone with the suffering, and I didn't know how to pray about it. Soon I became sick about becoming sick.

The "break" came one morning while I was eating breakfast with my mother. When I told her how I dreaded math class, she suggested I try imagining Jesus was there with me. We didn't often talk about religion, though she talked about it a lot with her sisters and friends. Ordinarily, I would have written this off as "mother talk," but this day a place deep inside of me went "click," and I was suddenly different.

I thought about it all the long bus ride to school. By the time I got to math class, I had decided that Jesus would stand behind the teacher, just a hair to the left of her. She would ask me, "What is two plus two?" and I would tell my answer to him. The teacher would not know; I would seem to be looking at her. I trusted

Jesus. He would never humiliate me. I would have an ally there with me; I wouldn't be alone anymore.

"You, what is two plus two?" She was looking at me. I tried it. I looked past her. He was there. I had a hard time answering. She went on to other kids. I kept watching Jesus, though, wondering if the others knew he was there. I had not succeeded in answering, but I now had a secret—a wonderful, positive secret—and something to think about other than my sick stomach. Imagining Jesus and having my secret became a reason to look forward to math class.

The next day I tried again. Within that week, things were stirring. I could talk when the teacher spoke to me. I could find the answer. The Jesus of my imagination always had the consideration to wait while I calmed down and looked for the answer in my mind. He never jumped in and said, "How come you don't know that?" So I began to look forward to Jesus "teaching" math. Within two weeks, everything was different. I was healed.

I don't recall being sick for a long time after that. And suddenly the teacher was kind to me and only me. For the rest of high school that teacher became the first person I would ever have as a genuine colleague. I had been healed, and the healing did much more than make math class bearable. Humiliation and faintness of spirit had been replaced by honor and strength and the power of lasting, deeply mutual relationships.

It occurs to me now that another healing—one for the teacher—might have taken place as well. Imagining Jesus with another person is a wonderful healing prayer for him or her. I didn't know this at the time, and it was probably beyond my comprehension then. But as Paul writes in Romans 8:26-27, "We do not know what we ought to pray for, but the Spirit himself intercedes for us. . . . The Spirit intercedes for the saints [that is, believers] in accordance with God's will." I imagine that some deep inner hurt within that teacher was the real source of what seemed to a teenager to be meanness. She certainly didn't manifest any such meanness or inner hurt that I could see after this experience. It may be that the Lord took me up on my imagination prayer in more ways than I knew.

For some time after this healing, I assumed I had done a neat trick of imagining. But in adulthood, when I tried to imagine Jesus in difficult situations, somehow I couldn't. I thought, oh, for a child's imagination! But when I began to read about positive imaging, about Jesus, and about inner healing, I knew that it was only partly my imagination. Jesus has said he would be with us always. I had acknowledged his presence with me, and that acknowledgment had opened a door. He had been out there waiting for me to open it.

The function of the Holy Spirit within us is to witness to the reality of Jesus in our lives. The power of the Holy Spirit within me had made all of this possible. Without knowing it, I had turned over my inner hurts to the working of the Spirit.

The downward spiral started by the divorce was stopped there. The Lord had somehow managed to place my father within me and to address and heal the deepest heartache I had. There were no more missed school days, no emotionally caused upset stomachs, no such fear as I had had in that class, and no more of the inner shock that the divorce had caused. No mere imagination can do that.

What did actually happen?

1. I acknowledged that I was hurting and needed some help.

2. I asked Jesus into the situation.

3. I embraced the state of expectancy. I did not look for a solution or a change; I was just so happy Jesus was there with me that I was glad for whatever would happen. I could have prayed for healing specifically, but that did not occur to me. However, my determination to converse with Jesus whenever the teacher addressed me was a prayer-in-action for the healing of that relationship.

Those are actually the major steps required for inner healing. Through them, I was able to become strong enough to let go. I could stop being my own sole defender and stop "grinding" inside about the deeper losses of my family life. I was also released to forgive my parents, partly by understanding that they were victims of the situation too and partly by having another source of inner worth that allowed me to be generous with love.

I now realize that I was always the temple of the Holy Spirit. I had simply, innocently, unknowingly made the tiniest bit of room for the Lord to do some work in one of his own temples. As Paul writes, "If the Spirit of him who raised Jesus from the dead is living in you, he will also give life to your mortal bodies through his Spirit" (Romans 8:11). That Spirit had been living in me. He who raised Christ from the dead had given me a whole new life, within myself, within my family, and out in the wider world.

Prayer Starter

Identify a place of inner hurt within you. It may be an observable situation, as with my math teacher, or it may be something deeper inside.

Imagine yourself in that situation. Very deliberately place Jesus in the picture. Let the situation unfold in your mind and see in what direction it will go.

Alternatively, when you find yourself in a situation of hurt, quietly bring Jesus into the picture, there with you. Be sure not to let people see any religiosity; this will seem fake and be far from healing. Let this be a secret between you and the Lord. Keep on doing this as long as the situation persists and see whether it doesn't change.

This is a long-accepted technique for inner healing. (Notice that this is a form of positive imaging.) However, some people do not find it easy to visualize in this way. If you are one of them, simply ask the Lord (in words) to come into the given situation and be there with you. Then let it go. He will be there.

In any case, you probably will not know anything different is happening or feel any different—until the situation actually changes. Then don't forget to thank the Lord, even, or especially, if it looks as if the change is just a coincidence.

Chapter 14

Shattered Spirits,
Hungry Lives

Shattered spirits, hungry lives—there are so many among us. I once knew a woman who for forty years was a very active member of her church. She also had an active social life with the church members, who would come to visit her in her beautiful house while her husband was at work. Her husband, prominent in town, had never been a member of the church or active in any religious organization. When he died, the entire town turned out for the funeral. And then the entire church, the entire town, stopped visiting her.

What's so different, she wondered. I'm in my same house, I still like to entertain, I still go to church, and my husband is still not with me when I do these things. But suddenly it's as if I don't exist. I'm not part of the town or the church anymore, no matter what I do, because I'm a widow. You'd think they would come more often. But now, there's nobody, ever.

This woman experienced a deep, soul-emptying need for love, for affection, for an affirmation of her personal worth. She was surrounded by apparent wealth, but emotionally and socially, she was running on empty. Unfortunately, many widows and divorced women go through this transformation of becoming socially invisible. Of course, this type of loneliness—the kind that can only be filled humanly with physical presence and with emotional warmth—happens to men, too, but the simple fact that women tend to live longer makes it more prevalent among women.

This type of emptiness is so prevalent that it is a very good metaphor for the human condition. Loneliness is only one face of the emptiness. The real problem is that nothing in this world is permanent. You cannot count on anything or anybody on this earth, and if that is your only source of fulfillment or of self-worth, it is all over right now. "Running on empty" is not just something that happens to widows. It is what happens to any-one who feels truly alone, for any reason at all—depression, ill-ness, a major life transition, or anything else that makes one feel isolated.

That is the bad news. The good news is that this is just the underside of a God-given, built-in, and vital-to-life human capac-ity, the spiritual equivalent of the instinct for self-preservation. It is the need for the one who will always love, the one who gives us our worth from the very moment of our conception. That one, of course, is God, and we have direct access to God in Jesus Christ.

If you are among those "running on empty," you are in very good company, included among them, Paul and the other apos-tles. Most people think of Paul, even in his early life as Saul of Tarsus, as being on top of the world. As he describes himself in his letters, he was a Jew of Jews, a lawyer of lawyers, a Pharisee of Pharisees, educated under the top legal expert of his day, Gamaliel. He had had every advantage, as we would say. When he quit that career to become an apostle, it seemed he went straight to sainthood. Most of us don't even get one great career. This guy got two!

Except that wasn't the way it was. Paul too had a shattered spirit and a hungry life. If we look underneath the veneer, we see that he had a whole life of suffering. His encounter with Jesus on the road to Damascus was a watershed experience, but on either side of it, he suffered.

Before it, he must have suffered in spirit. Many people of his age were, like Paul, determined to live a perfect, law-of-Moses-abiding life. He felt compelled by his religious perfectionism to cause destruction and misery to the Jesus people. He must have been searching desperately for some way to gain God's approval as well as to stamp out what he felt was a threat to his own religious way of life. After his conversion, Paul suffered in many other ways, including physically. He describes these sufferings in several places, including 2 Corinthians 5:3-10.

Before his conversion, Paul was in need; afterward, he was fulfilled. In between, in the story of his conversion, we can find the key to overcoming the shattering and disillusionment of our lives. Look at the needy Paul before his conversion. By saying Paul was in need, we are not saying being Jewish was a bad thing. Paul never gave up his love of Judaism, as is evident in some parts of Romans. The reason he wanted to search out the renegade sect of Jesus people was that, at bottom, he had a powerful hunger for God. He desperately searched the Scriptures to find out how he could be more and more perfect in the sight of God and desperately tried to be good enough to ensure that God would not reject him at the judgment.

So he studied harder, practiced the Jewish law more rigorously, and tried to make everyone else do so too. Like an alcoholic or a depressive who goes to school to study psychology, becomes a great therapist, and yet finds himself still an alcoholic or a depressive, Paul was finding out that human effort was just not sufficient. He was "wound too tight" and something had to give.

The cure, the assurance of salvation, is not in a book. It's not in a list of rules, in perfect attendance at Sunday school or synagogue, or in anything we can do at all. As Paul himself later wrote, "All have sinned and fall short of the glory of God" (Romans 3:23). No one "gets it right" before God, not completely.

The cure is in the encounter with God, the acknowledgment of utter helplessness before God. For Paul and for Christians it is in the encounter with Christ, the very Christ Paul had been avoiding and whose followers he had tried to destroy. Paul had read about God's love, but as with any other love, he didn't know it until he met its source on the road that day. After that, his hungry-for-God life was filled up and his shattered spirit at peace.

But first his old life was shattered. He was thrown off his horse, blinded, and terrified by the encounter. His whole concept of himself was gone. He was in utter darkness for three days, like Jesus in the tomb. Then, like Jesus resurrected, he was set free, healed, and given real purpose in life and real assurance of God's presence, genuine access to God forever.

A healing occurred in this story, and the nature of that healing is central. Ananias, a Christian, was sent by God to Paul. He laid hands on Paul, saying, "Jesus . . . has sent me so that you may see again and be filled with the Holy Spirit" (Acts 9:17). Paul was physically healed, but the more important healing took place within. The Holy Spirit was working within him. For Paul, that was the fill-up. It was also the source of years and years of preaching and healing and apostleship to come.

It is important to notice that this change did not mean there was no more suffering. It meant his suffering had a purpose. Also there is an irony here. Before his conversion, the Jews liked him and the Jesus people feared and hated him. Afterward, some of the Jews hated him, the Gentiles (then the pagans) did not know what to make of him, and the Christians did not trust him.

Look what happened to him in consequence. In the conversion story itself, the Lord says to Ananias, "I will show [Paul] how much he must suffer for my name" (Acts 9:16). In 1 Corinthians 4, Paul tells us some of what he has been through: "To this very hour we go hungry and thirsty, we are in rags, we are brutally treated, we are homeless. We work hard with our own hands. . . . We have become the scum of the earth" (4:11-13). He was shipwrecked, publicly whipped, run out of town and left for dead. But what does he do in response? Listen: "When we are cursed, we bless; when we are persecuted, we endure it; when we are slandered, we answer kindly" (1 Corinthians 4:12-13).

How? Why? Paul sees himself this way: "I bear on my body the marks of Jesus" (Galatians 6:17). Paul also writes, "If anyone is in Christ, he is a new creation" (2 Corinthians 5:17), and he knew that because it applied to him. His life was transformed. Suffering and hunger and all manner of earthly emptiness—these things themselves were transformed. What made the difference? Not comforts, for sure. Not social acceptance. Not a sense of personal perfection. Being filled with the Holy Spirit, healed in God's love, made the difference. And it all happened as a result of the encounter with Jesus on the road to Damascus.

Not all of us get a dramatic experience like that. But all of us can have the assurance of God's love and be filled with the healing power of the Holy Spirit. The widow at the opening of this chapter began to express her love of people, God, and nature by creative projects, and that self-expression, for God's sake, filled her up. For her, this was a way of allowing the Spirit to live and speak within her. After a while, people started coming to see what creative thing she had done now—after her emptiness had been filled in their absence.

We cannot be "too bad" for God to use us and fill us up. Paul was responsible for many people being jailed, and he assented to the murder of Stephen. But in Paul's new life, God still used him for a great purpose.

An acquaintance of mine, Park, had that kind of healing—the kind that takes you from nothing to everything, from running on empty to a full spiritual tank. He was an elegant man, a Ph.D. psychologist, and an excellent therapist who helped many, many people. He also happened to be gay. This was long before homosexuality was an acceptable topic of conversation in most places, and most people were far less educated about that subject than they are today.

Park began coming to the church I attended. On the day of the annual parish meeting, when tensions within the parish manifested themselves in a prolonged silence, Park decided he would take the floor if nobody else wanted it. He would express his appreciation for the church and tell those gathered what had brought him to this point in his life.

Park explained that he had always known he was gay. He had tried to find the right relationship. He had tried many relationships. None of them made him feel fulfilled. Then he had tried going to school to study psychology. He had done very well and had made a good profession out of it. But studying psychology had not explained to him how to have a full life in his relationships. In fact, what he had learned about himself was just how hungry he was and just how shattered his spirit was. He could not find a way to fill up or bind up his shattered heart; he was so alone.

After many years, he one day opened the New Testament and started reading about Jesus. It occurred to him that Jesus also was single. He never in the whole of the Gospels had a romantic relationship. But Jesus still had purpose and was beloved by God. Park had an inspiration. He would be like Jesus. He would stop looking for relationships and for fulfillment and acceptance in this world. He would take his worthiness from the image of Jesus and be as much like him as he could. From that day on, Park had remained celibate. But his life had been filled up. He had worth and purpose, and he knew himself to be nothing less than a son of God.

Am I recommending his healing for everyone? No. Am I advocating gay rights or celibacy? I am not advocating anything—except Jesus. This was Park's healing, in Park's time. But look what happened. He had been running on empty and, as with the widow, there was no earthly person or thing that could bring him fulfillment. But the encounter with Jesus "on the road"—as he wrestled with his sufferings—made all the difference. If you have ever had a shattered spirit or if your life is hungry, maybe you should just see where Jesus is on the road you happen to be taking in your life today.

Prayer Starter

Read the Gospel of Mark. Read it slowly and deliberately, all the way through, though it does not need to be all in one sitting. Keep at it every day until you have finished a thoughtful reading.

Notice two things. First, Mark emphasizes miracles and Jesus' defiance of evil and sickness.

Second, Jesus has many relationships with different people, some enduring and some momentary. The most lasting of these friends, the disciples, always seem to misunderstand what Jesus tries to teach them. Jesus seems to have no really satisfying relationship for any extended period of time—except one. What keeps Jesus going? Hint: What keeps him going is not the miracles; they are the result, not the source, of what he does to keep in touch with his sense of self and his sense of purpose.

What keeps Jesus going? Prayer.

Chapter 15

Arise and Shine: A Burst of Joy for the Brokenhearted

How many of you have never grieved? Probably no one. Virtually everyone has experienced devastating loss of one kind or another. Did you know that for grief the Bible promises a double healing? First, the grief itself will be healed, and second, we are promised a burst of joy. One of the Bible's figures for grief and loss is "thick darkness"; the healing is characterized as bright light. We ourselves are to "arise and shine." All of this is meant for today. This is also one of the promises of the second coming, when the Lord pierces the thick darkness of the sin of the world for the last time and his own light fills the world.

We need this promise of healing. The thick darkness can hit us at any time. At a party, I was asked to make friends with a lovely little lady who didn't seem to know anybody. I wasn't particularly comfortable just spending time with this one person; I thought I should be circulating. But I spent an hour trying to make her happy. As it happens, it was the last hour of her life. She was killed in an auto accident on the way home from that party. What if I hadn't thought it was important to comfort her and help her to the full joy of that gathering? It disturbs me deeply to think I might so easily have denied her that. The grief becomes very personal—even though I had not known her very well.

In speaking about grief, however, I am not just talking about the death of a loved one. How many of us have lost jobs or whole careers? A middle-aged executive with a Ph.D. in nuclear physics was a successful administrator for a huge company. Then another company bought it out, and his job was eliminated. He was unable to find another position. Fortunately, he had invested wisely and could live on those investments, but his thick darkness was visible. It was the grief over the lost career and over the way in which he himself had been "thrown away" after so many productive years.

Other losses are just as devastating, such as the loss of physical faculties. Older members in my parish increasingly grieve over being too frail to come to the church to worship anymore. Often such losses are accompanied by depression, a thick darkness.

We are all in some kind of darkness at some time. At those times, it may feel as if God has abandoned us. When we lose a loved one, we also tend to feel abandoned by that person—even though we know that in most cases it was not his or her choice to leave us. And we are in despair because humanly our loss cannot be fixed. We are captives to the human condition and to our individual pain.

Grief and the healing of grief of all kinds are clearly represented in the Bible. The Bible depicts literal grief and God's promise of healing for it. While he is on the cross, Jesus brings the healing of loss to his mother by asking his disciple John to take care of her (John 19:25-27). Before Mary's son dies, she is given another son. Clearly Jesus cares about loss and grief. Jesus weeps upon seeing Lazarus's tomb—and then calls him forth to resurrection (John 11:33-44). Notice that even with Jesus, grieving coexists with faith, resurrection faith. The more we care for God and our fellow human beings, the more likely we are to grieve.

In the Bible, grief is also used as a metaphor for the sense of isolation that comes from feeling abandoned by God. The particular grief addressed in this way is Israel's feeling that God had abandoned them during the Babylonian captivity. They had abandoned God first, to be sure; but they had repented, and Isaiah (chapter 40) had told them that they had been forgiven. Still, they grieved over the loss of Jerusalem and their temple. More than repentance was needed to heal their sense of loss. This type of healing comes about by a sovereign decision made solely by God, without people's deserving—that is, by grace. And that is what happened: God declared that by his own gracious gift, Israel's loss would be filled. They would get back their city and temple and a double portion of God's own favor—plus joy!

This relationship between grief and grace is very poignantly addressed in Isaiah 60–61. He spoke there to the captive, but he also speaks to us today, because we too are all at one time or another in our own version of darkness. Isaiah says, "The Spirit of the Sovereign Lord is on me, because the Lord has anointed me to preach good news to the poor. He has sent me to bind up the brokenhearted . . . to comfort all who mourn, and provide for those who grieve in Zion—to bestow on them a crown of beauty instead of ashes [that is, anguish], the oil of gladness instead of mourning, and a garment of praise instead of a spirit of despair. . . . Everlasting joy will be theirs" (Isaiah 61:1-3, 7). This promise is both for the healing of grief over such things as death and for the healing of the sense that God has abandoned us—the healing of the deep darkness of body, mind, and spirit, the darkness that comes with any severe loss. This healing is God's own choice for us. The key is that the Lord comes to us, in the midst of our despair. The darker our darkness, the brighter his revelation.

Whether we have been distanced from God in some way or our darkness is the result of a loss in this world, the revelation of God's presence and the healing are ours, by God's own design. So how can we have this joy for ourselves? The first answer is this: the joy of the Lord is not a human emotion. We may or may not feel emotion along with it, but this particular joy is one that comes from God. In a sense, it is his joy over us. The second part is that only God can accomplish such a healing. We can cooperate with the Lord, though. We do this by refusing to take our darkness and despondency as the index of God's love for us or of his presence with us. The two are not related. God is always with us.

Our assignment as Christians is to believe, first and foremost, that the Lord will come again. So, in the long term, there is the greatest of hopes. In the meantime, we are to know that the Lord really does see and care about the weight of grief, illness, or depression that sits upon our soul. We are to hang onto God's caring no matter how long it takes (see Romans 14:8). The point is to belong to the Lord through it all.

Notice that I said, "Through it all." I did not say we are going to feel better right away. We might. We might not. Most people praying for healing hold tightly to the healing rather than to God. They focus on the what, when, and how of the healing rather than holding onto God and belonging to him, which is the core of healing. Whatever happens after that becomes a part of belonging to God. If we really leave the visible outcome to the Lord, we are more likely to get a healing of the kind we wanted in the first place.

Let me tell you about two healings from thick darkness of different kinds, before I tell you about my own healing. In one of my churches, one of the regular attendees was a teenage girl who never said anything at all. She seemed intent on not attracting any attention to herself. At one of our healing services, I asked whether anyone wished to tell about healing they had experienced during previous services. To my enormous surprise, this teenager, who had always been so shy, got up in front of everyone and said, "I was healed from depression. I was in real darkness, and nobody knew, but I was healed, and all because you all prayed for me in that last healing service." I was shocked. I had had no idea.

Another healing from a physical "thick darkness" occurred during a healing service at that same church. The highest lay official in our parish, the senior warden, had a grown daughter who was in her late twenties and had been an established professional. Now, though, the daughter had developed an inoperable brain tumor; she was nearly blind. I had laid hands on her and prayed for her at the family home about a month before. Now the senior warden and his wife had brought their daughter to this healing service. When it was time, the three of them came up for healing prayer.

At the altar rail, her father said plainly and simply, "Her tumor has been healed. There is no sign of it anymore; the doctors verified it. Could you heal her blindness now?" I was grateful that her "inoperable" tumor had been healed, evidently through prayer, and intimidated that the healing of the related blindness should be brought to me in such simple faith.

I prayed, "Lord, please heal this blindness" (thinking, "Oh, Lord, I can't do anything; won't you please do something?"). Here, again, is that old dichotomy: I knew my own helplessness and also the graciousness of the Lord. I wanted so much for that grace to be manifest right then for this young woman, but I couldn't command it to be so. We could only wait upon the Lord.

Two days later I came home to a message from the senior warden. His daughter had driven the family to the shopping center, so it seemed she was going to be OK. Her blindness had been healed. "We know you didn't do it," he added. "The Lord did, but thanks for the prayer." After that, on a regular basis, they called to report her further progress. She got a promotion at her job. She got her own apartment. She got married. And on and on.

The daughter had been healed from thick darkness of the most literal kind. She had been healed from the loss of her career, the loss of her vision, and the potential loss of her life. The parents had been healed of the impending loss of their daughter. They were more than grateful. Their fear and grief had been turned into nothing less than joy.

My own healing from thick darkness had a powerful element of the joy of the Lord in it. It came after my mother died, when I had accepted a new church in another state and was so worn out and busy with moving and a new church that I never stopped to think about grief.

You know I believe in resurrection. I didn't begrudge my mother hers. I was genuinely happy for her. But grief is not supplanted by faith; they are not at odds with each other. Grief is a hole in the soul, a place forever empty in the griever. Thus we can know both at the same time.

My mother had died in December. It was now late spring, and I had gotten some respiratory illness that wouldn't go away. I couldn't clear my sinuses. I could hardly talk. I couldn't sleep.

At that time a neighboring church was conducting a conference on healing, led by a guest speaker. I really wanted to hear him and I was scheduled to help with parts of the conference, so I dragged myself there. On the last afternoon, the minister of the church, the guest speaker, and I were to be available for private counseling and healing prayers.

No one came. Having nothing else to do, the three of us started talking about my cold. The visitor kept prompting me to say more about it. I could hardly talk, but I tried to accommodate him. After a while he said, "You know, the more you talk about your cold, the more you say about your mother. Would you mind if I prayed for you about losing your mother?" So the other two ministers laid hands on my head and prayed about the cold and about losing my mother. I can't remember any one thing they said. But it went on for some time.

Then all of a sudden I began to laugh.

That sounds irreverent, doesn't it? But it didn't feel that way. I wasn't laughing at anything. I was just laughing—from somewhere deep inside. It felt so good, like being filled with warm honey. Then the other ministers began to laugh too. We laughed and laughed and laughed. We laughed until we were worn out.

My sinuses were clear. My cold was gone. The laughing had cleared out what medicines and weeks of attempted rest could not. And from that moment, the cold never came back.

More important, a palpable weight had lifted from me. I hadn't known there was a weight because I hadn't felt it arrive. I had just been carrying it like a huge bag of wet sand. That weight was grief as well as a spirit of despair, an all-pervading despair that had seeped into everything. It had literally made me sick. But it was gone. Ever since that day I have only a sense of wholeness when I think of my mother being with the Lord.

That night I went to the healing service. People were slow to accept the invitation to prayer, so the ministers asked me to recount the story of my healing that afternoon. I did. At that point, my own congregants had had no experience with spiritual healing. However, they asked me to retell the story in church the next morning.

There was still more going on within me. For a while I couldn't figure out what had happened. It still sounded so irreverent, to God and to my mother, that I had laughed like that. I searched the Scriptures for an explanation. Why laugh? To be sure, just as Isaiah had said, I had, in a burst of joy, experienced the healing of grief, loss, and captivity of spirit. Then one day I came upon something like what I had experienced. It was in the Beatitudes, in Luke 6:21: "Blessed are you who weep now, for you will laugh." I had experienced Jesus' own promised healing of grief, in a burst of laughter and of joy that was far more than human.

Whatever breaks our heart or breaks our spirit, God sees it. God cares about it. But we have a tough assignment: to see and love God back, to arise and shine in the very midst of thick darkness. We don't have to feel it. We just have to act on it, in whatever way we can make God more and more the center of our life. The glory of the Lord is promised to us, and the kingdom, after all, is really almost come.

Prayer Starter

On a dark day—dark weather, dark emotions, whatever is your own darkness at the moment—do something loving for someone else. Pray for them. Send a card expressing concern for them. Or—the most effective of all—smile, deeply and genuinely, at someone whom you absolutely cannot stand or who cannot stand you. Then say hello and walk away. This is prayer in action. Your actions celebrate God's love. You will have penetrated thick darkness to find God. Then say a quiet prayer in words or envision the light of the Lord around the other person. This brings the task out of the realm of the merely human and into that of true Christian spiritual healing.

Instead of trying to ignore your darkness or just get through it, face into it. Speak to it as if it were a person. In the midst of the full realization of your darkness or grief, praise God. Praising God is a joyful thing to do; it will eventually bring you joy. But more important, you are defying "thick darkness" with an affirmation of the glory of the Lord and a claim to your part of that glory. This is another way to penetrate darkness to find God.

Chapter 16

Vindication

Many years ago I saw a movie about a farmer, his wife, and their three little children. They wanted to buy a farm, but they couldn't afford it. So they rented a run-down, falling-apart old farm from a man in town and arranged that if they did well and fixed up the place, then at the end of a year they could buy it.

These people were so poor that the children didn't have shoes and they didn't have enough to eat. But the parents saved and worked and fixed up the buildings. At the end of the year, they had brought in a good crop and the farm was in better shape than it had been for many years. They were very proud of it. All of the hardship and all of the sacrifice had been worth it.

The farmer went to see the owner, ready to conclude the deal and buy the farm. But the owner had already been by to see exactly how good that farm looked now.

"You can't afford to buy the farm," he sneered. "It's worth twice what it was last year. Besides, I've already agreed to sell it to somebody else."

The farmer had no choice but to go back and tell his wife the terrible news. He couldn't stop grinding about it in his stomach or aching about it in his mind.

In the next scene of the movie, the farmer was in the barn working. He looked up to see the owner walking by, looking at the property. The farmer picked up his gun and aimed at the owner, finger on the trigger, ready to shoot. Right then his three-year-old daughter ran by, in the path of the gun. He hesitated for just a moment . . .

Do you think he shot the owner? Do you think he should have? Do you feel maybe it was wrong, but the owner deserved it anyway? Whatever else you think, you must understand how bitterly that farmer needed vindication. Why vindication? It was as if God or the cosmos had decided to punish the farmer for all of his hard work rather than to reward him. All of us can connect with that. All of the people of God are in need of vindication. This need is a defining characteristic of the people of God.

Ray, one of the lay leaders in a church where I was pastor, lost his job at the bank. Why? Because our church had bought a small piece of land for a parking lot. It just happened to be a plot the bank manager wanted to buy too. So the angry manager took out his feelings on the nearest employee from that church. Ray sued. The case was in court for years, for so long, in fact, that I never heard how it came out. But by then, real vindication was out of reach. Even if Ray were to win the case, he could never work at that bank again. He had had to find a new job in the meantime. And now he had all of those legal fees. Such is, humanly speaking, the condition of the people of God.

The sense that we did nothing wrong and yet the world just crunched us up into bits anyway—this is something we all have shared. We know bad news and ill health and taxes and frustration of every kind. The question that hovers is always this: Why us? What, if anything, did we do to deserve this? The answer may well be, nothing.

This human condition is the effect of the sin of the world. In the New Testament, this condition often is referred to with a legal metaphor. The metaphor consists of the false accusation or unfair punishment of God's people, their need for an attorney, and the defeat of the false accuser. That is why the New Testament refers to Jesus as our advocate. Listen to 1 John 2: 1-2: "If anybody does sin, we have one [in many translations, "an advocate"] who speaks to the Father in our defense—Jesus

Christ, the Righteous One. He is the atoning sacrifice for our sins, and not only for ours but also for the sins of the whole world." We suffer evil at the hands of the rest of the world—not just as the result of our personal sin—and Jesus is bringing this unjust situation before God.

Jesus is our heavenly attorney, defending us against the undeserved punishment of the way it is to live in this world. He is the only one who can mount a defense and finally accomplish our deliverance. The sufferings and the evil of the world are embodied in a figure we call Satan, which means "accuser"—specifically, the bringer of false accusation. To speak of Satan is to acknowledge that our suffering is brought about by a massive spiritual force, one that is much bigger than we are and that we cannot fight directly. That is why it takes Jesus to defend us. That is why the people of God need vindication.

This brings me to the reason I have called this chapter "Vindication." Vindication has two meanings. The first is an act of proving that we have been falsely accused of something. Vindication has the connotation of defending a person against critical attack (of any kind) and implies proving the unfairness of such an attack.

The second sense of the word is an equally important one. According to a variety of dictionaries, vindication also means insisting on the recognition of something, for example, one's rights. The Latin word from which vindicate derives is actually closer to this second meaning. The Latin word *vindex* refers to a "protector." The related Latin verb *vindico* means first "to liberate or deliver" and only secondly "to avenge." Our vindex cleans up the injustice done to us by the false accuser Satan.

This sense of our relationship with God is a powerful theme throughout the Bible. God does not just execute judgment upon people. That's only a small part of his overall task of maintaining cosmic justice. Much of the Old Testament refers to the larger task of protecting God's people by calling God "Deliverer" or "Helper." Israel was always appealing to the Deliverer, specifically the one who delivered them out of

Egypt, out of Babylon, out of the wilderness, and out of the hand of an enemy (or the enemy, Satan).

Whatever oppresses us, however unfairly the world has dealt with us, the cause of it is not God judging us unfairly or abandoning us. The sense of unjust loss and of hopelessness should be our cue to go to God the advocate, God the deliverer. While we should not put up with evil, we should not engage in evil in defending ourselves. (Of course, self-defense is not evil.) Whatever else we do, we mustn't forget to turn the resolution of our situation over to the Lord. To do this, it helps a great deal to know for sure that God really does have a soft heart for our personal situation. He really is there to heal, help, and deliver us from whatever oppresses us.

Here is an example: when my mother prayed for people, things happened. People used to come to her for prayer all the time. One day during the Vietnam war, a young, recently married couple came to see her. The husband, Bill, was a marine and had just received his orders to go to Vietnam. He knew this happened to a lot of young people then, but to him his going seemed particularly unjust. Bill had been adopted at birth. For all these years, the idea that his real parents had given him up had been grinding in his stomach. His mother had rejected him and sent him away. He couldn't get past that. It was so unfair. It felt as if he had been judged unworthy to be her son before he even had a chance to do anything at all. Finally, now that he had the chance to form a family of his own, he had to leave and face the front line. He might never come back. It was as if the Father in heaven had abandoned him twice over. He hadn't done anything to deserve this. His heart needed healing badly. His family needed healing too, but he didn't know it yet.

My mother prayed for the couple. After a while, she said, "Go to the hospital chapel, the one with the beautiful stained glass. Go down front and pray and thank God for Vietnam."

"Thank God for Vietnam?" Bill objected. "Not on your life!"

"I'm sorry," Mother replied. "I prayed, and that's what came to me. And that's all I've got."

Bill and his wife weren't at all happy with that, but they were desperate. So they finally reasoned, why not? What could happen? It was, after all, only a prayer.

So they went to the hospital chapel, went down to the front, and, as hard as it was, they thanked God for Vietnam. Once finished with praying, they turned to leave. As they turned, they realized that another couple had entered and were sitting in the back. The husband also had on a Marine uniform. He was clearly an officer.

The two couples began to talk. When they realized that both men had orders to ship out to Vietnam right away, they became more interested in each other. The officer took out some family pictures. "I don't have any except this one of my mother," Bill said. He took out his birthmother's photo, the only thing he had of hers, and gave it to the officer. "I was adopted," Bill explained.

"That can't be your mother," said the officer.

"Why not?"

"Because . . . that's my mother."

It turned out the two were in fact brothers and the mother had had to give up Bill for good reasons. In the end, through that unwilling visit to the chapel, the biological family was reunited. The officer requested that Bill work with him in Vietnam, and during that tour of duty they got to know each other better. Both returned—Bill to be reunited with his wife, and with the family that God had given him.

Notice what happened here. Bill's orders to go to Vietnam brought his already keen sense of the unfairness of life to a sharp focus. Things looked desperate, and up to the very last minute, it seemed God had abandoned him twice over. But God can use anything for good (Romans 8:28), and in this case, God used what seemed to be the very worst situation to bring about the very best. Notice that the whole character of what happened was of healing—the healing of Bill's family and a deep inner healing of Bill's own heart. In thanking God for Vietnam, Bill and his wife invited the Lord into their particular situation, thanked him in advance for the good he would bring out of it, and further, however unknowingly, accepted the Lord as their only possible advocate. The Lord himself fought the injustices brought upon Bill through the sin of the world. Those injustices were then replaced by joy and honor. Finally, Bill was given a knowledge of himself as a person who was loved by family and by God. That is vindication.

Who gets vindicated? How do you get this type of healing for yourself? Believe God's promise of help, no matter how distant it looks and no matter how foolish it feels to believe. Look evil in the face and know it and nevertheless act upon the Lord's word. Let Jesus be your advocate, your helper, your healer. If you can allow him in just a little to do this, then another member of the human race will have acknowledged the Lord as our only defense against the sin of the world and will have given him dominion over suffering.

Prayer starter

Read Romans 8:28. Take the very worst thing in your life, and pray to God,

> *I know that you hate the evil and harm the world does to people. I also know that you can use anything at all for the good of the person who loves you. Therefore I thank you for this situation—not because you sent it, but because of the good you are going to make out of it. Thank you, God, for the vindication of your people and for the healing of my situation. Amen.*

Chapter 17

Resurrection Tree

"Kamila, the man from Nazareth is planting resurrection over your mother's grave!" Electric shock went through me. I could feel it running up and down my arms, straight into my heart. We were planting an olive tree on my mother's grave in Israel, and this was the answer to years of prayer. It told me that there is a loving Lord who is always with us. It also ushered in a new depth of healing experience for me.

My mother had nurtured me all the way to my recent ordination as an Episcopal priest, and I had wanted to give her something back, something that would last for life. So I had taken her on a tour of Israel, a trip she had always wanted. I never guessed the trip would constitute the rest of her life. I never guessed I'd have a "baptism to undergo" (Luke 12:50), in more ways than one. The trip, and her death, would be the ultimate challenge to my resurrection faith.

The trip, and her death, were to be the ultimate challenge to my resurrection faith. The death of my mother was also the one event in my life that most powerfully connected the healings I had experienced in this world with the ultimate healing of resurrection. A healing-of-life—my life—also was incipient in this experience. Ever since then, I have been a changed person, with the power of the Holy Spirit actually moving me to new places and entirely new avenues of creativity.

It was a miracle that my mother took the trip to Israel at all. It was notoriously difficult for anyone to get her to leave home for anything. She would always say, "I never go anywhere unless the Lord himself sends me a ticket." We didn't have money for the trip, either. I prayed for it anyway. Almost immediately, I found out that a missionary organization was about to lead a trip for clergy and their spouses that even I could afford. Though Mama wasn't clergy, at seventy-three she had put in a quarter century of leading people to the Lord. She was always telling people how she had been "called" by the Lord, and it was contagious. I told the society about her, and they said she could go.

When she heard about the trip, even she had to admit that the Lord was giving her a ticket. So in December 1984 we flew to Israel.

We were both in good spirits, and she had always been in good health, albeit with some aches and pains. That's what made it so curious that a sort of theme song began to run through my head, virtually from the moment we took off. It said, over and over, "You'll be all right without her." The message really did have the numinous quality of some of the Bible stories in which the Lord speaks to someone. It also delivered a very serious emotional punch. Her death would be, for me, different from any other death. Relatives with whom I had been close had died before, but I had always had a deep peace about it. It was as if I had had all of those relationships I could have on this earth—a full plate, a cup running over. But with my mother, I had been so close to her that I was actually afraid I could not live a normal life when she was gone. Our feelings were locked together very strongly.

All of this was complicated by the fact that I, like everyone else we knew, used to ask my mother to pray for every need. My mother would receive guidance that was sometimes surprising, almost always frighteningly accurate and very powerful. We were all totally dependent upon her for spiritual support. It was like having a hotline to the Lord, a sort of red phone available at all hours for emergencies large and small. With such powerful interconnections between Mama and me, it seemed as if my life would fall apart if she were not there.

We arrived in Israel and immediately found Jerusalem to be enthralling. Our Israeli guide took us up Mount Zion. Mama and I walked the Mount of Olives, pungent as it was with her favorite wild rosemary everywhere. At the base of the mount, at Gethsemane, I saw my first olive tree, a tree held by the local people to be a living symbol of the resurrection, a "resurrection tree." It was then I found out why the olive tree lives for so long. An original olive tree puts out shoots all around its base, then dies. But the shoots grow up and have shoots and so on for a thousand years, making a wider and wider "tree." Thus an olive "tree" can almost live forever.

When we left Jerusalem, we headed to Galilee. I had asked to be baptized in the Jordan River, and that had been scheduled for the day after we were to arrive in Tiberias. Because the river was on the way, however, the tour director asked, as we passed it, if I would do it right then—dark, cold, and rainy though it was at that moment. The other clergy kept telling me you can't be rebaptized. But they didn't understand. I wanted with everything in me to experience, literally to be immersed in, something Jesus himself had experienced. So I decided, yes.

Even in growing darkness the site was beautiful, with overhanging trees and stone walks. Nothing could discourage me, not the freezing water, not the continuing rain. I explained my desire for the baptism to the other clergy, and their attitude changed. They decided to do it up right. Someone got out a prayer book and recited the whole official baptism service while I started into the river. Though I was sure I was about to suffer hypothermia—with teeth firmly gritted—I allowed a colleague to push my head under the freezing water. As I came up, I heard him say the final words of our baptism service: "You are sealed as Christ's own forever."

Someone on the bank shouted: "Look at her face!" All of our tour companions were there, staring at me—all except my mother. Where was she? But I didn't have time to dwell on that. At the very moment I had come up out of the water, something like a spiritual Niagara Falls had fallen upon me, filling me with the absolute certainty of the presence of God—

and with heat. I became physically very warm and remained warm for hours, even though I was by now standing, all wet, in the cold air and rain. Most important, however, were the words that came into my heart—not out loud, but unmistakable, and definitely not my own: "Don't worry about your mother. I will take care of her now."

(I should explain that the experience of physical heat often accompanies a miraculous healing. The "Niagara Falls" experience—being filled with a great whoosh of what felt like liquid hot honey inside—is often called baptism in the Holy Spirit, or an infilling of the Spirit.)

Mama had remained on the bus; she was the only dry one. That night, with a great feast at the hotel in Tiberias, we all celebrated the baptism and the new life it brings. We were all transported by the experience at the river. We were deeply connected and full of the joy of the Spirit. Later, I went to sleep in the room I shared with Mama. The peace was thorough and solid, as if I were insulated from the noise of the world by a thick but beautiful wall. For the first time during the trip, worries about my mother were laid to rest. The inner voice had stopped.

I woke up early, still enveloped in a palpable peace. I was alone. I was certain of that even before I opened my eyes. Was Mama out for a walk? No, that was not her style. Was she at breakfast? No, she would have wakened me. What then? Only that I was alone, bathed in a tangible soft wind of the Holy Spirit. I got up and looked out over the Sea of Galilee. It was completely lifted out of the earthly, covered in a mist glowing with a rose-pink light. It was dawn.

Then I saw her. But it wasn't my mother. It was what she would have called a husk—just the earthly part. She had died during the night. Paramedics later said she'd had a heart attack.

One thought intruded upon the peace that was still so much with me: "Is that all? After a whole life of resurrection faith, is that it?" This sight of the husk-left-over, physically so close to me and formed like an abandoned cocoon near me while I was sleeping, forced upon me a concrete knowledge of my own mortality.

Would I be just a husk some day? This pit-of-the-stomach, physical knowledge of death planted itself in my heart—even as the full significance of the previous events was becoming apparent. I had had clear guidance the whole way. God must have cared about me and about her.

Our tour group gathered on the hotel terrace overlooking the Sea of Galilee, and someone began to read Mark 1:16-17—the passage immediately after the baptism of Jesus: "As Jesus walked beside the Sea of Galilee, he saw Simon and his brother Andrew. . . . 'Come, follow me,' Jesus said, 'and I will make you fishers of men.'" "See, Kamila," the reader said, "the Lord called your mom in the same place where he called his first disciples." That's when the electricity began. It changed our whole mood. I made a decision then and there: we would bury her here, overlooking the sea. And that is exactly what we did, at Magdala, in what is known as the Scottish Mission cemetery.

It was only afterward that the full significance of the burial became clear. First of all, I discovered that if I had decided to take her home, it would have cost thousands of dollars, many weeks, and the services of international attorneys. Second, you can't just bury a Gentile and a foreigner in Israel; you need special permission from the government in Jerusalem. Third, even with permission, the paperwork and legalities are staggering. There is a major religious and cultural difference between Israel and the United States. In Israel, you can't even take a casket for granted. They bury the dead the same day they die, in a shroud, just as in the Bible. Someone would have to be found to make a casket.

The whole thing was made downright frightening the next day when we finally arrived at the United States embassy in Tel Aviv. The staff there refused to give us any aid because it was after 4:00. They were closed. Then numerous other problems arose, including word that, for our transactions at the embassy, only cash was accepted. We had to deplete our entire group's resources to pay them.

At the moment when I made the decision to leave my mother in Israel, I anticipated none of these problems. What I did know was that these twenty people had come to Israel—most of them for the only time in their lives. We were supposed to go on the boat trip across the Sea of Galilee that day. It was going to be a few hours before we would know any more about how to proceed with the burial. So I said, "Let's go on the boat trip anyway. We might as well celebrate the Lord while we have to wait." I also thought it would be a good place to pray, sitting in the middle of the sea, hearing about all of the places on the shore where Jesus carried out his ministry.

We arrived at the boat two hours late. But the owner was actually relieved. There had been a problem with the motor, and it had just been fixed that very moment. So we went across the sea, finally arriving some hours later at Capernaum. I literally rode and walked in the steps of Jesus that whole day, albeit in a daze.

In the meantime, the tour director and the bus driver were glad for our absence; they were trying to make arrangements. While we were gone, they were finding out all of the impossibilities of the situation. Nevertheless, at about 4:00 that afternoon, when we were due back, they drove to the hospital where Mama had been taken. They were held up by a very slow car ahead of them that went all the way to the hospital too. The driver turned out to be the official from Jerusalem, bearing—miraculously—the papers giving permission for the burial. At the moment when they arrived there, a truck pulled up from the opposite direction. That driver, a carpenter from Nazareth, had just finished making the casket.

And so it was at that about 4:30, as the sun was beginning to set, we all converged at the Scottish Cemetery, on a hill overlooking the Sea of Galilee. There we held the burial.

A few hours later, I was on the plane home, enveloped in the deep peace of the Holy Spirit and cushioned in the faith of twenty other ministers. But in the pit of the stomach, the image of the husk was still there. How could I ever really preach resurrection again? The double experience I'd had—grief and God, husk and holiness—did not resolve for two years.

During those two years, I asked the Lord a pointed question: "Why do you build into the system that the closest relationship one ever has, has got to end?" I never expected to get an answer, but I did. I had moved to a new place, where I knew no one and faced many difficulties—all of which would have been all right if I could have called my mother for assurance and prayer. But for the first time ever I could not call her. Slowly I came to realize that my own guidance was just as strong, in its own way. I began to realize, too, that although I had never known my father, who died two years after my mother, there were many things I could only have received from him, many wonderful things. That is another story altogether, but let me just say this: having never known my father, I had not known at least half of the resources with which I had been born. I did not know to look for them until I was forced by the circumstances to find new strengths within myself.

Then I found that far from being alone, I had both parents and their strengths firmly planted within me. They were both a part of me. I could not lose them. I began to come into my own in my clergy career and so—looking back upon it—I can genuinely say that from the day of the baptism, I had begun a whole new life. I myself had experienced a resurrection.

As my own strengths began to emerge—some I had never known before—the answer to my question to the Lord came to me: It is not that your mother is taken away; she herself has a new beginning. But you, also, have a new beginning. There are aspects of yourself, your calling, and your spirituality that would never have had freedom to emerge while your mother was your ideal. It is not that there was anything wrong with her spirituality. You simply never looked beyond her, to the future within you. The Lord wanted you to do just that.

Thus the Lord had set me up for the conclusion of the events of my mother's death. Two years after her death, I had another chance to go to Israel with many of the same people. The guide for this tour was a Christian man from Nazareth. I had resolved, if possible, to go and put a stone on my mother's grave. The minister at the Scottish Mission had the stone made, and when it was time for our service, he brought with him an olive sapling from his yard. He noted that it would be a fitting symbol of resurrection to plant that tree at the gravesite.

Our service for planting the stone was all very ceremonious, except for one thing: that olive tree would not be planted. Each of us took a turn digging the rocky ground and not even a pencil hole could be made in it. Time was passing, and we were all sweating and uncomfortable as to how to end the ceremony under these circumstances. That was when the guide from Nazareth stepped up. He made just one stroke with the shovel and planted that tree, firmly and beautifully, with all of us looking at him as if he had made a mountain move.

Then it was that I heard those words. "Kamila, the man from Nazareth is planting resurrection over your mother's grave!" Then it was that my sense of this whole experience resolved itself. Yes, we are a husk. Yes, that's what we leave behind. But that is not all there is. There had been too many signs and too many wonders for me to deny that somehow, anyway, there is a God and there is more to this life than what we leave behind it.

The death was real. The Spirit was real. The resurrection was real. I could face my congregations and preach the resurrection with faith renewed. I did and still do to this day. I had thus had a healing of faith, one that I had never known I would need.

Healing comes in many forms. This one formed me as an independent person, one who could do ministry in the power of the Holy Spirit. So many aspects of faith healing were contained in this series of events that I can only stop and look with wonder.

As we have noted previously, any genuine healing cascades to other people. This one has. Ever since the burial, many Christian tour groups have stopped at my mother's grave to see where the man from Nazareth left his mark and to get close to the woman who had had this blessed death. Sometimes they call me afterward or send a photograph, and I can tell that they have been deeply and positively affected by this part of their pilgrimage. I believe that some of them have also had experiences of healing in connection with it. But one thing I know: my mother is still speaking her message of unconditional commitment to the Lord Jesus Christ through the many people who have visited the site of what my uncle called my mother's "elegant death."

Prayer Starter

Do not ever prejudge the nature of a healing. God is really God, the sovereign Lord, the Lord of Hosts, Adonai Sabaoth. C. S. Lewis, in his children's books about Narnia, uses a lion as a figure for the Lord. One of the characters describes that lion as "not tame." He mustn't be taken for granted. On the other hand, he is not far off, and he sees and feels every bit of pain and suffering as if it were his own. It is his own, because we are his own. Be still for a moment, and know that he is God.

In the stillness, try this prayer:

O, my God, there is a God. Help me, Lord, and do it as the Sovereign of my life. Amen.

Then stand back. And wait in a spirit of expectancy, for whatever—whatever—the Lord might choose to do with his own creation—you.

Chapter 18

The Bottom Line

The preceding chapters contain many stories of healing as well as examples and suggestions about praying for yourself and for others. Here I want to summarize the thrust of those examples. Then, taking the prayer of Jesus at Gethsemane, I will adapt the prayer started from "Finding the Father in Heaven" to show the ways in which it illustrates these cardinal points of healing prayer. Examples of ways in which you might use it to pray for yourself and others are then given. Perhaps when you reach the end of the chapter, you will pray some part of this prayer, or one like it, along with me, and say with me at the end, "Amen."

Some Things Not to Do

1. Do not make yourself the center of attention by praying fancy prayers or by emotionalism; the Lord should be at the center always. See Matthew 5:5-8.

2. If you are praying with someone else, do not tell the person what to pray for unless you have listened sensitively and actually heard that need in their own words. Do not give advice, either. The other person is there for divine, not human, intervention and is probably quite desperate to get to the real thing.

3. Do not mistake your own emotion for the operation of the Holy Spirit. The Lord may be working without your sensing it. Above all, the Lord's work does not depend on you or on your

perception of his presence. Thank God! Though you have no power at all, you have the power to bring about miracles, because you can call upon the Lord—and leave it to him.

Some Things to Do

1. Prime the pump as you continue to develop in healing faith— learn how to pray when you cannot pray or when you simply need a fresh start (see, for example, chapters 4, 7, and 11). Aids for making yourself more ready and open for prayer often include:

a. General housecleaning and forgiveness (chapter 3)

b. Reading Scripture in some regular pattern or as part of specific types of prayer (chapters 6, 7, 12, 13, and 16)

c. Praise and thanksgiving (chapters 6, 8, 9, and 16)

d. Christ-oriented positive imaging—keep the focus on the Lord, not on yourself; on well-being, not on illness (chapter 13)

2. Adopt an attitude of expectancy. Be like the baby at the breast, innocently expecting to be fed, yet knowing yourself to be at the total mercy of your mother God (chapters 2 and 17).

3. Be specific, simple, and direct in your request. You are inviting the Sovereign Lord to take dominion over that particular area of your life (chapters 9 and 13, among others).

4. Never give up. You may be desperate, but that doesn't mean you have to be deprived. Total desperation is often the pre-condition for spiritual healing (chapter 6, among others).

A Model Healing Prayer

Let's look at a modified form of the prayer exercise from chapter 7 (and based on Mark 14:32-36) that makes the above steps explicit. (The core of the prayer is as follows, but you may be inspired to use the situation and prayer in Mark in other ways.)

Abba, Father, everything is possible for you. Take this cup from me. Yet not what I will, but what you will.

If you have read or heard the Gospels, you know that Jesus is already in tandem with the Holy Spirit; he prays regularly, he clearly knows Scripture very well, and he praises God for God's works. Thus he has already "primed the pump." In this prayer:

1. Jesus adopts both a spirit of expectancy and God-oriented positive imaging. He does this in several ways:

a. He is obviously suffering, yet puts his mind firmly on God.

b. He acknowledges his own hopelessness and prays from the midst of it.

c. He states his attitude of expectancy ("everything is possible"); he assumes God will bridge the gap between earth and heaven, hopelessness and healing.

d. He addresses God as "Abba, Father." He speaks as if God is very close; he is.

2. Jesus asks for what he needs in specific terms (deliverance from the "cup," meaning his crucifixion).

3. Jesus gives everything over to God, no matter what the outcome. He does not give up but gives the situation over to the Lord.

Of course, Jesus does die; but then he (and because of him, we, too) receives the most unexpected and world-shaking healing of all. God did, after all, answer his prayer. The "cup" of death was taken from him, and incipiently, from all of us, as well. Thus this prayer not only is a model for our own healing prayer, but it is also the promise of God's answer to all of the rest of us.

Using the Model

How might you use this model? Remember that you might substitute the name of a friend in the places where the prayer below refers to oneself. Such a prayer may be used with the other people or in their absence.

Reread Mark 14:32-36. Choose one area of desperation or general need in your life. Pray using Jesus' words, adapting them to your situation. The Lord has a very particular empathy with anyone who needs this prayer! (Remember his own words from the cross, Matthew 27:46: "My God, my God, why have you for-saken me?" He experienced severe desperation before God answered him.)

If you can visualize, "see" Jesus there with you also praying for you. If you can't bring up a mental vision of him, begin by asking him to be there with you. Then pray (for example):

Abba (Father, Mother, Lord—whatever form of address is comfortable for you), everything is possible for you, and I expect and await your entry into this situation. I thank you and praise you in advance for whatever is your will in this. Now, Lord,

—I have suffered a miscarriage and want so much to have another child; I picture that new child in my arms, as the one I lost is now in yours.

—I am smoking too much and no matter how hard I try, I cannot stop. I ask you to heal me by whatever means you wish, through a physician, through a medication, through a direct mir-acle. I picture myself strong and breathing deeply of the clean air of the Spirit.

—I am drinking too much and cannot stop. I know you are the only one who can help me. Help!

—I am alone in my life and ask for a husband/wife/best friend. Please lead that right person to me.

—I am unable to rise up from the depths of depression. I cannot picture myself in a state of well-being, and I cannot imag-ine that you can help. But all things are possible with you. Will you please take over?

—I desperately need a job. Find me and find my place in the world. Let me be a praise to your name in that place.

—(And even this:) I am happy in my life and want to use it for you. Place me wherever you would have me, for your sake.

I thank you in advance for hearing and answering my prayer. In the name of the Lord Jesus Christ. Amen.

Postscript

As I spent the weekend reading the final proofs of this book, I had an experience with which I would like to leave you. At the beginning of the weekend, I began to have an increasingly painful toothache, but I continued to read these stories anyway. In the growing pain that day, I asked myself: "What if I were one of you, reading these stories in this much pain, and someone told me that the Lord is working on my healing even though I can't feel it now? Wouldn't I just throw the book down?" By Saturday night, I was awake with constant pain. My toothache had grown into a serious crisis. Experience had taught me that this particular pain meant I'd need a root canal.

On Sunday, as I continued to read these stories of the Lord's intervention in my life, my tooth began to feel less painful. By Monday morning—when the book was ready to be mailed—all of the pain was gone. When I went to the dentist's office on Monday, the dentist said the fracture lines in my tooth were superficial. I wouldn't need a root canal, and the tooth was permanently fixed in a half hour.

I knew before I reached the dentist's office, however, that my tooth had been healed. It was a double healing—of the human kind and of the divine kind. It was a double healing in another way, too—of the pain and of the experience and expense of the root canal. Did this book heal me? No. But dwelling for a whole weekend in the Lord's presence helped. I can genuinely attest to you that the Lord is still working on keeping me whole, and he is working within you, too.